Get Connected ...
Explore ...
Succeed!

D1535726

Open Book Companion Website

www.longmanesl.ca/gaetz.cw

Improve your English skills:

✓ **Interactive activities to practise the four skills: reading, writing, speaking, and listening**

✓ **Vocabulary review exercises for each chapter**

✓ **Variety of exercise types: fill-in-the-blank, matching, multiple-choice**

✓ **Model essays, summaries, and oral reports**

✓ **Links to websites related to the content of each chapter**

English Skills

Second Edition

Open Book

Lynne Gaetz

PEARSON
Longman

To access
the Companion Website

Step 1 Go to **www.longmanesl.ca/gaetz.cw**

Step 2 Choose **Open Book**.

Step 3 When asked, enter the following username and password:

Username ob39247   **Password** wrmpee

Step 4 Follow the instructions on the screen.

Technical Support: tech@erpi.com

7963

English Skills

Open Book

Second Edition

English Skills

Open Book

Second Edition

Lynne Gaetz
Collège Lionel-Groulx

COMPANION WEBSITE BY
BRENT DAVIS REID
Collège de Bois-de-Boulogne

PEARSON
Longman

DISTRIBUTED IN CANADA BY ERPI
5757, RUE CYPIHOT, SAINT-LAURENT (QUÉBEC) H4S 1R3
TELEPHONE: **(514) 334–2690 ext. 232**   FAX: **(514) 334–0448**
infoesl@erpi.com   **w w w . l o n g m a n e s l . c a**

ACKNOWLEDGEMENTS

I would like to express sincere thanks to:

- Lucie Turcotte for her patience and insights while editing this book
- Sharnee Chait and My-Trang Nguyen for their invaluable editing
- Dominique Gagnon and the team at Dessine-moi un mouton
- Brent Davis Reid for his wonderful work on the companion website
- Rebeka, Diego, Dominique Brown, and Nick Forrestier for being such willing models during our photo shoots
- Mawlid Abdul Aziz and Martin Neufeld for their interviews, and Liz Gagnon for her transcripts
- My students and colleagues at College Lionel-Groulx
- My colleagues throughout the province who kindly provided feedback:

Nancie Kahan (Cégep de Saint-Jérôme)
Carol Lakoff (Collège de Maisonneuve)
Mary Lise Lavallee (Collège Ahuntsic)
Marc Tousignant (Cégep de Sherbrooke)
Marie White (Collège François-Xavier-Garneau)

Finally, I extend special thanks to my husband and children.

Managing Editor
Sharnee Chait

Editor
Lucie Turcotte

Copy Editor
My-Trang Nguyen

Proofreader
Katya Epstein

Art Director
Hélène Cousineau

Book Design
Dessine-moi un mouton
Pige Communication

Cover and page layout
Dessine-moi un mouton

CREDITS

The following authors, publishers and photographers have generously given permission to reprint copyright material.

Chapter 1 p. 1-16 Photograph of desert © Tomasz Resiak / iStockphoto. p. 4 Photographs of guitar, cow, and prairie © Jupiterimages; photograph of boots © Joy Prescott / iStockphoto; photograph of football © Dusty Cline / iStockphoto. p. 8 "Confessions of a Messy Person" by Dorothy Nixon reprinted with permission; photograph of chair, courtesy of the author. p. 11 Video segment "George and Rosemary" © National Film Board of Canada; illustrations by Jérôme Mireault. p. 13 Photograph from *Silent Night,* reprinted with permission of Muse Entertainment; photograph of the "Hugger Busker" by François Miron, from *Hugging Life,* a book by Martin Neufeld.

Chapter 2 p. 17-33 Image of man juggling from Photothèque ERPI. p. 19 "Too Busy to Sleep" by Nancy Hellmich, originally published under the title "A Teen Thing: Losing Sleep" © 2000, USA TODAY. Reprinted with permission. p. 23 "Juggling Acts: A Day in the Life" by Naomi Louder reprinted with permission. p. 24 Photograph of alarm clock © Jupiterimages. p. 28 "I, Telemarketer" by Eugene Henry reprinted by permission of the author. p. 31 Video segment "Lies, Myths and Downright Stupidity" © ABC News.

Chapter 3 p. 34-48 Photograph of bungee jump © Matej Michelizza / iStockphoto; photograph of young people courtesy of the author. p. 37 Photographs of kewpie doll and CB radio © Dorling Kindersley; photograph of hula hoop © Jupiterimages. p. 38 Photograph of boufant hairdo © Topfoto / PONOPRESSE; photograph of zoot suit © Underwood Photo Archives / SuperStock; photograph of platform shoes © Jupiterimages. p. 39 Photograph of man sitting on a flagpole © CORBIS / Bettmann; photograph of man swallowing a goldfish © Topfoto-UPP / PONOPRESSE; photograph of phone-booth stuffing © CANADIAN PRESS / Rex Features (2005), all rights reserved. p. 41 Photograph of extreme cyclist © Marianne Badiola / Camera Press / PONOPRESSE. p. 44 Video segment "Second Life" © Canadian Broadcasting Corporation. p. 45 "My Bad Google" by J. Kelly Nestruck originally published under the title "How One Man Cleaned up His Sordid Internet History" in *National Post*, March 13, 2006. Material reprinted with the express permission of National Post Company, a CanWest partnership. p. 48 Photograph of young people courtesy of the author.

Chapter 4 p. 49-65 "Blue Dancers" (1897) by Edgar Degas (1834-1917, French). Pastel. State Hermitage Museum, St. Petersburg, Russia. © Bridgeman Art Library, London / SuperStock. p. 52 Self-portrait of Vincent Van Gogh © Jupiterimages. p. 53 Vincent Van Gogh`s bedroom in Arles (1889) © Jupiterimages. p. 55 Photograph of Frida Kahlo and Diego Rivera © Topham / PONOPRESSE. p. 56 Photograph of a woman watching a painting by Friday Kahlo © James Veysey / Camera Press / PONOPRESSE. p. 59 Video segment "A Brief History of Reggae" © Annenberg Media; photograph of Bob Marley © Peter Mazel / London Features / PONOPRESSE. p. 61 Photograph of Jim Carrey © Yoram Kahana / Shooting Stars / PONOPRESSE. p. 64 Photograph of John Lennon and Yoko Ono © Allan Tannenbaum.

Chapter 5 p. 66-78 Photograph "Belgium, Binche, carnival of the Gilles" © Joern Sackermann, Germany. p. 68 Photograph "Holi Festival, Girl with Colored Powder on Her Face" © Dinodia / Omni-Photo Communications. p. 72 Photograph of Mogadishu © De Agostini Editore Picture Library. p. 76 "Naming Good Path Elk" by Kenneth J. Kline reprinted with the permission of *Essence* magazine.

Chapter 6 p. 79 Photograph "Business Traveller" © David Crockett / iStockphoto. p. 81 Photograph of Asian puppets © Ingram Publishing / SuperStock. p. 83 Photograph of cobra © iStockphoto. p. 85 Video segment "Inside North Korea" © ABC News; photograph of Kim Jong-Il © Gamma / PONOPRESSE. p. 86 "The Grand Canyon" by Andrew Wells reprinted with permission; photographs of shoe sole and big horn sheep © Jupiterimages; photograph of ridge top buck © Dave Raboin / iStockphoto; photograph of farm track © Duncan Walker / iStockphoto; photograph of mountain ridge © Richard Elliot / Topfoto / PONOPRESSE. p. 87 Photograph of Grand Canyon © iStockphoto. p. 90 Illustration by Jérôme Mireault.

Chapter 7 p. 93-108 Photograph of window seat © Diane Diederich / iStockphoto. p. 94 Photograph of poker game © Jason Lugo / iStockphoto; "Sports and Life" by Jeff Kemp reprinted by permission of the author. p. 95 Photograph of football helmet © Jupiterimages. p. 102 "Out of Sight" from *Cockeye* by Ryan Knighton. © Ryan Knighton, 2006. Reprinted by permission of Penguin Group (Canada), a division pf Pearson Canada Inc. p. 103 Photograph of white cane © Karin Lau / iStockphoto. p. 107 Video segment "The Big Snit" © The National Film Board of Canada.

Chapter 8 p. 109-121 Photograph of traffic lights © Pixtal / Superstock. p. 110 Excerpt from "2005 Crime Trends," from Statistics Canada publication "Juristat," *Crime Statistics in Canada 2005*, Catalogue 85-002, Volume 26, Number 4, pages 3-4, released July 20, 2006. p. 112 Photograph of jaywalker © Photolibrary. p. 113 Photograph of woman showing her driver`s licence © Nancy Louie / iStockphoto. p. 115 Video segment "Road Rage" © Canadian Broadcasting Corporation. p. 120 "The *CSI* Effect Has Juries Wanting More Evidence" by Richard Willing © 2004, USA TODAY. Reprinted with permission; photograph of gavel © christine balderas / iStockphoto.

Appendix 3 p. 141 Illustration by Jérôme Mireault. **Appendix 5** p. 143 Photograph of dresser © johanna goodyear / iStockphoto; photograph of bed © Richard Hoffkins / iStockphoto; photographs of closet, faucet and stove © Jupiterimages.

Preface

Designed for high-beginner to low-intermediate students of English as a second language, *Open Book English Skills*, Second Edition, is a comprehensive integrated skills text.

The Second Edition, visually enhanced in four colours, includes eight chapters focusing on contemporary themes linking reading, listening, writing, and speaking skills. High-interest readings are in a variety of reading styles including interviews as well as narrative, persuasive, and informative essays. Reading activities are diverse and contain everything from standard vocabulary and comprehension exercises to verb hunts, pair or team work, summaries, and "make your own question" activities.

Listening activities always start with two exercises that develop a skill such as pronunciation followed by an authentic interview relating to the content of the chapter. The Second Edition contains many new video segments to stimulate discussion and enrich students' understanding of the topic.

After the eight chapters, you'll find Writing Workshops, an expanded writing section providing students with strategies and extensive practice in building better paragraphs and essays. Workshops can be assigned at any time during the semester as a reference to the writing topics found in each chapter.

On the inside back cover, there is a paragraph and an essay checklist. Encourage students to get into the habit of consulting the relevant checklist before handing in written work. They can verify that their text has the proper structure. They can also refer to these checklists when they do peer editing.

A new exciting feature is the Open Book Companion Website. Throughout the chapters, you'll notice links to the website where students will find extra information, vocabulary-building exercises, and activities to practise the four skills. There is also an extensive Teacher Section containing reading and listening tests, transcripts for the audio and visual material, and additional teaching tips.

This book contains more material than is necessary for a 45-hour course, but the extra material provides the flexibility to offer different readings during different sessions. Additionally, chapters can be presented in whatever sequence you prefer.

Complementing this book is *Open Book English Grammar*, Second Edition, which contains exercises that are based on typical student errors. Explanations are clear, and grammar exercises contain interesting biographical and historical information.

Highlights

Warm Up

Each chapter begins with a meaningful activity to prepare students for the topic while activating prior knowledge.

Reading

Students learn strategies to improve vocabulary and read effectively.

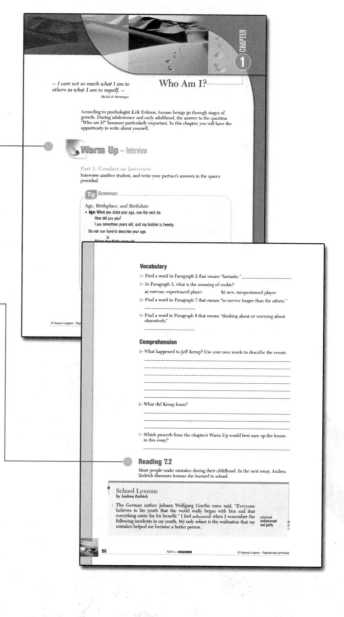

-- I care not so much what I am to others as what I am to myself. --

Michel de Montaigne

Who Am I?

CHAPTER 1

According to psychologist Erik Erikson, human beings go through stages of growth. During adolescence and early adulthood, the answer to the question "Who Am I?" becomes particularly important. In this chapter, you will have the opportunity to write about yourself.

Warm Up -- Interview

Part 1: Conduct an Interview
Interview another student, and write your partner's answers in the spaces provided.

Tip Grammar

Age, Birthplace, and Birthdate
- **Age:** When you state your age, use the verb *be*.
  How old are you?
  I am seventeen years old, and my brother is twenty.
  Do not use *have* to describe your age.
  ~~is~~
  ~~Alissa has thirty years old.~~

Vocabulary

1- Find a word in Paragraph 2 that means "fantastic." _____

2- In Paragraph 3, what is the meaning of *rookie*?
  a) veteran; experienced player   b) new, inexperienced player

3- Find a word in Paragraph 7 that means "to survive longer than the others." _____

4- Find a word in Paragraph 8 that means "thinking about or worrying about obsessively." _____

Comprehension

1- What happened to Jeff Kemp? Use your own words to describe the events.
_____
_____
_____
_____

2- What did Kemp learn?
_____

3- Which proverb from the chapter's Warm Up would best sum up the lesson in this essay?
_____

Reading 7.2
Most people make mistakes during their childhood. In the next essay, Andrea Zedrick discusses lessons she learned in school.

School Lessons
by Andrea Zedrick

1 The German author Johann Wolfgang Goethe once said, "Everyone believes in his youth that the world really began with him and that everything exists for his benefit." I feel ashamed when I remember the following incidents in my youth. My only solace is the realization that my mistakes helped me become a better person.

ashamed embarrassed and guilty

86   PART 4 -- DECISIONS   © Pearson Longman -- Reproduction prohibited

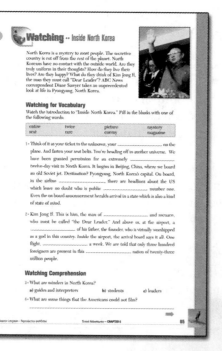

Watching -- Inside North Korea
North Korea is a mystery to most people. The secretive country is cut off from the rest of the planet. North Koreans have no contact with the outside world. Are they truly uniform in their thoughts? How do they live their lives? Are they happy? What do they think of Kim Jong Il, the man they must call "Dear Leader"? ABC News correspondent Diane Sawyer takes an unprecedented look at life in Pyongyang, North Korea.

Watching for Vocabulary
Watch the introduction to "Inside North Korea." Fill in the blanks with one of the following words:

| entire | twice | picture | mystery |
| seat | rare | enemy | magazine |

1- Think of it as your ticket to the unknown, your _____ on the plane. And fasten your seat belts. You're heading off to another universe. We have been granted permission for an extremely _____ twelve-day visit to North Korea. It begins in Beijing, China, where we board an old Soviet jet. Destination? Pyongyang, North Korea's capital. On board, in the airline _____, there are headlines about the US which leave no doubt who is public _____ number one. Even the on board announcement heralds arrival in a state which is also a kind of state of mind.

2- Kim Jong Il. This is him, the man of _____ and menace, who must be called "the Dear Leader." And above us, at the airport, a _____ of his father, the founder, who is virtually worshipped as a god in this country. Inside the airport, the arrival board says it all. One flight _____ a week. We are told that only three hundred foreigners are present in this _____ nation of twenty-three million people.

Watching Comprehension
3- What are *minders* in North Korea?
  a) guides and interpreters   b) students   c) leaders

4- What are some things that the Americans could not film?

© Pearson Longman -- Reproduction prohibited   Travel Adventures -- CHAPTER 6   85

Watching

Interesting video segments from authentic sources enrich students' understanding of content while building language skills.

Speaking

Speaking activities ranging from discussion to interviews and presentations help students communicate confidently.

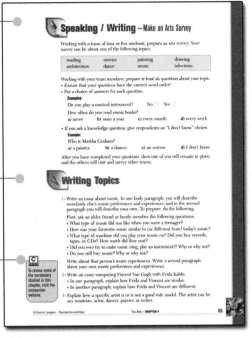

Writing Topics

Challenging writing topics allow students to practise different writing patterns and integrate content.

 Extensions and practice activities help students consolidate what they have learned.

Listening

Each chapter includes a listening exercise to develop skills such as pronunciation, recognizing numbers, identifying verb tenses, and forming questions.

Students listen to authentic interviews from CBC and NPR to expand their spoken and written expression.

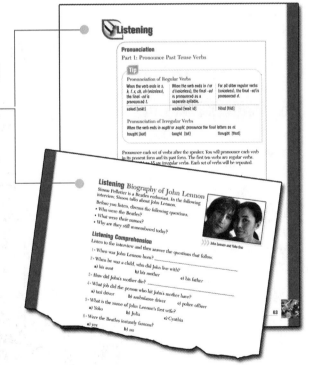

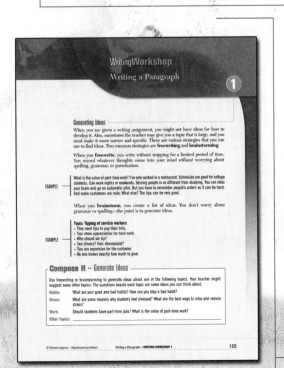

Writing workshops provide students with strategies and extensive practice to build better paragraphs and essays.

Scope and Sequence

	READING	WRITING	LISTENING/WATCHING
PART 1: LIFESTYLE CHOICES			
CHAPTER 1 **Who Am I?**	• Identify main idea and supporting details	• Write paragraphs using the present tenses	• Listen to phone messages • Listen for main ideas • Watch a video
CHAPTER 2 **Balancing Act**	• Use context clues to understand vocabulary • Identify main and supporting ideas	• Complete a survey • Write an essay • Write a journal	• Listen to verbs ending in -s or -es • Listen to an interview • Watch a video
PART 2: POPULAR CULTURE			
CHAPTER 3 **Trends**	• Recognize cognates • Comprehend main ideas • Identify bias • Do team reading	• Write interview questions • Write an essay • Summarize main ideas • Make an arts survey	• Listen for main ideas • Watch a video for main ideas • Identify information about extreme sports
CHAPTER 4 **The Arts**	• Identify main ideas • Synthesize information • Do pair-reading	• Write questions • Write a paragraph based on partner's responses • Write an essay	• Listen for main ideas • Watch a video • Identify biographical information
PART 3: CELEBRATIONS AND TRAVEL			
CHAPTER 5 **Traditions and Celebrations**	• Use a dictionary • Identify main ideas	• Write a short paragraph • Write definitions • Write a summary • Write an essay	• Listen for main ideas and details • Listen to words containing *th*
CHAPTER 6 **Travel Adventures**	• Scan for information • Do team reading • Identify main idea and understand details	• Write questions • Write a short paragraph • Write an essay • Prepare a brochure	• Listen for main ideas and details • Watch a video for main ideas
PART 4: DECISIONS			
CHAPTER 7 **Life Experiences**	• Identify main ideas and understand details • Read actively • Identify the message	• Write questions • Write a short paragraph • Write an essay • Support opinions	• Listen to words containing *h* • Listen for main ideas • Watch a video
CHAPTER 8 **Legal Limits**	• Scan for information • Identify statistics • Read actively for main and supporting ideas	• Write questions • Write an essay	• Listen for main ideas • Watch a video for main ideas

SPEAKING	VOCABULARY	GRAMMAR
• Share information • Interview a partner • Pronounce numbers • Pronounce sentences	• Learn personal identification terms • Learn new verbs related to habits • Identify context clues	• Form questions • Practise subject-verb agreement • Learn some capitalization rules
• Pronounce verbs ending in *-s* or *-es* • Interview a partner • Describe a place	• Tell the time • Learn work-related vocabulary • Identify context clues	• Form present tense questions • Practise subject-verb agreement
• Discuss photos • Ask and answer questions • Present a trend	• Use descriptions • Learn about product, activity, and fashion fads • Identify numbers	• Use present progressive • Practise using adjectives • Form questions
• Play an arts trivia game • Discuss issues • Present a biography • Pronounce past tense verbs	• Learn art-related terms • Describe objects • Define words	• Write past tense questions • View verbs in context
• Pronounce *th* • Interview a partner • Discuss issues	• Learn names of holidays • Learn synonyms • Define words	• Form questions • Practise present, past, and future tenses
• Interview a partner • Discuss issues • Make a presentation about travel	• Learn travel-related vocabulary • Learn country names • Follow directions	• Practise using modals (*should*) • Form questions • Give advice
• Discuss issues • Present a true story	• Learn common proverbs • Learn descriptive vocabulary	• Review verb tenses • Practise using personal pronouns • Form questions
• Discuss issues • Ask and answer questions • Do role-playing	• Learn crime-related vocabulary • Learn driving vocabulary	• Form questions • Form negatives • Review verb tenses

Scope and Sequence

Table of Contents
Open Book English Skills, Second Edition

Who Am I?

•• I care not so much what I am to others as what I am to myself. ••

Michel de Montaigne

According to psychologist Erik Erikson, human beings go through stages of growth. During adolescence and early adulthood, the answer to the question "Who am I?" becomes particularly important. In this chapter, you will have the opportunity to write about yourself.

Warm Up •• Interview

Part 1: Conduct an Interview

Interview another student, and write your partner's answers in the spaces provided.

> **Tip** Grammar
>
> Age, Birthplace, and Birthdate
> - **Age:** When you state your age, use the verb *be*.
>   How old **are** you?
>   I **am** seventeen years old, and my brother **is** twenty.
>
>   Do not use *have* to describe your age.
>   is
>   Alison ~~has~~ thirty years old.
>
> - **Birthplace:** Describe where you were born using the past tense of *be + born*.
>   Where **were** you **born**?
>   I **was born** in Halifax.
>
> - **Birthdate:** There are two ways to describe a birthday. Notice that months always begin with a capital letter.
>
>   *on* + month + day   *on* + day of month
>   Jeff's birthday is **on March 21**.   Jeff's birthday is **on the 21st of March**.

1 • What is your full name? _____

2 • What is your nickname? (A nickname is a special name used by close family and friends.)

_____

3 • Match the following titles with the appropriate people.

Mr. •   • Married women
Miss •   • All men
Mrs. •   • All women
Ms. •   • Single women

Which title is best for you?   Mr. ☐   Miss ☐   Mrs. ☐   Ms. ☐

4 • When were you born? _____

5 • Where were you born? _____

6 • What are you studying at college? _____

7 • Who do you live with? _____

8 • What are your hobbies? List two things. _____

Part 2: Introduce Your Partner

Now you and your partner should join a group of other students. Introduce your partner to them.

To practise your speaking skills, visit the companion website.

Tip

Introductions

You do not *present* your partner. You *introduce* your partner.

    Joan, I would like **to introduce** you to Samuel.

In social situations, you could say the following:

    Joan, I'd like you to meet Samuel. Samuel, this is Joan.

Reading

Reading Strategy

General Comprehension

Read the next essay so that you have a general understanding of its content.
• Do not use a dictionary.
• Do not stop reading when you come to new or difficult words.

Your goal is to understand the main messages of the text.

Reading 1.1

In the 1990s, a Canadian beer company made a very popular advertisement. In the ad, an ordinary-looking man explained what it means to him to be a Canadian. The "I am Canadian" rant led to a series of web-based rants about a variety of other topics. Here is an example:

I Am What I Am
by Jonathan McKay

I am not poorly educated. In fact, I studied horticulture at college.

I'm not a conservative or a **redneck,** and neither are my friends.

redneck
racist or narrow-minded person

I work with animals, but I don't smell like a pig, horse, or cow.

I don't eat beef seven days a week, although the beef from this region is really the best.

I don't chew pieces of hay. I chew gum like everyone else.

I don't wear **checkered** shirts or overalls, but I like a nice-fitting pair of jeans.

checkered
patterns of squares

I also don't wear a cowboy hat, but I have some fine cowboy boots, and I also wear rubber boots during the spring.

I own a big truck, but I also have a small car that I take to the city.

I believe my job is useful.

Workers like me provide you with the food on your table.

My job is great for the health. I spend a lot of time outdoors doing physical activities, and I breathe fresh country air.

I live in a beautiful region, and all around my house are wide-open spaces and the big blue sky.

I believe I have a great job.

My name is Jonathan, and I am proud to be a farmer.

Comprehension

1• Who is the audience for Jonathan's rant? _____

2• What are some stereotypes about farmers? Guess by looking at the information in Jonathan's rant.
   Example: They are poorly educated.

   _____

   _____

   _____

3• Why is Jonathan proud to be a farmer? Think of three answers.
   Example: He believes that his job is useful.

   _____

   _____

Writing ·· Write a Rant

You will now write your own rant. Before beginning, complete the following chart. As you put down each answer, think about some stereotypes associated with that category. For example, if you are male, what are some stereotypes about men?

I AM ...	STEREOTYPES
Gender: male ☐ female ☐	
Field of study: _____	
Home: city ☐ suburb ☐ town ☐ country ☐ farm ☐	
Part-time job:	
Marital status: single ☐ married ☐ divorced ☐ separated ☐ common-law ☐	

Now, on a separate sheet, write a rant about yourself. Explain things that are and are not true about you.
• Your rant should have at least ten sentences.
• Include a cover page for your rant. The cover page should give your name, the date, and a title. (The title could simply be "My Rant.") It should also have your personal coat of arms.
• Your coat of arms should be in the form of a shield. Decorate five parts of the shield with images that represent something about you. For example, if you are musical, you could insert a picture of a guitar. (The images do not have to be about things that you discuss in your rant.) You can include drawings or photos.

⟩⟩⟩ Jonathan's Coat of Arms

To read a teacher's rant, visit the companion website.

Exchange Rants

After you have finished writing your rant, exchange it with a partner. Write down the first ten lines of your partner's rant. Remember to change *I* to *he* or *she*. Also remember to change the verbs.

Using *Be*

Use the verb *be* to identify **age**, **hunger**, **thirst**, **feelings**, **height**, and **temperature**. Remember that the form of the verb must also agree with the subject of the sentence. To make the verb *be* negative, just add "not."

Steve **is** twenty years old. The weather **is** cold outside. They **are** not afraid.

Do not use *be* to express agreement.   I ~~am~~ agree.

Listening

Names and Dates

Listen to the following names and birthdates. Write the names and birthdates in the spaces provided. Each name and birthdate will be repeated.

Example: Name: *Marjorie* _____   Birthdate: *February 12, 1985* _____

Months

Review how to spell the months. Notice that the months are always capitalized.

January	April	July	October
February	May	August	November
March	June	September	December

1. Name: _____   Birthdate: _____

2. Name: _____   Birthdate: _____

3. Name: _____   Birthdate: _____

4. Name: _____   Birthdate: _____

5. Name: _____   Birthdate: _____

Pronunciation

Part 1: Identify *-ty* or *-teen*

Tip

Notice the difference between the pronunciation of words ending in *-ty* and *-teen*.

Generally, stress the last syllable of words ending in *-teen* and the first syllable of words ending in *-ty*.

She is fif**teen**.   She is **fif**ty.

Listen to each sentence. Circle the number that you hear. You will hear each sentence twice.

1. The shirt costs $(15/50).
2. She will turn (15/50) on her next birthday.
3. It is (13/30) degrees outside.
4. Louis is (14/40) years old.
5. We have $(16/60) left.
6. The temperature will rise to plus (13/30) degrees Celsius today.
7. Karen was born in (1919/1990).
8. I will retire in (2014/2040).

Part 2: Pronounce Dates

Pronounce each date after the speaker. You will pronounce each date twice. Notice which part of the word is stressed.

Example: Friday, No**vem**ber thir**teenth**.

1. Monday, April 30th
2. Friday, April 13th
3. Wednesday, January 12th
4. Thursday, August 31st
5. Sunday, July 1st

6. Saturday, October 25th
7. Tuesday, December 20th
8. Thursday, September 15th
9. Wednesday, February 18th
10. Monday, March 11th

Listening Telephone Messages

You will hear three telephone conversations. Complete the information in each memo.

CALL 1 *Job Application*

Name: Mr. ☐ Mrs. ☐ Miss ☐ Ms. ☐

First name: _____ Initial: __ Last name: _____

Marital status: single ☐ married ☐ common-law ☐ widowed ☐

Street Address: _____

City: _____ Province: _____

Phone number: Home: _____ Cellular: _____

```
┌────────────────────────────────────────────────────┐
│  CALL 2  Dental Appointment _____   │
│                                                     │
│  Name: _____    │
│                                                     │
│  Date of appointment: _____    │
│                                                     │
│  Time of appointment: _____                │
│                                                     │
│  Reason for appointment: _____    │
└────────────────────────────────────────────────────┘


┌────────────────────────────────────────────────────┐
│  CALL 3  Complaint _____  │
│                                                     │
│  Name: _____    │
│                                                     │
│  Telephone: _____           │
│                                                     │
│  Product: _____    │
│                                                     │
│  Model number: _____    │
│                                                     │
│  Date of purchase: _____              │
│                                                     │
│  Price: _____                                 │
└────────────────────────────────────────────────────┘
```

Reading

Reading 1.2

Dorothy Nixon, who is extremely disorganized, lives with a very tidy husband. When you read her essay, don't stop at unfamiliar words. Try to get the main ideas.

Pre-Reading Vocabulary

Before you read the essay, review the next words and their definitions.

- *Odd Couple*: *Odd* means "strange." *The Odd Couple* is a play written for the Broadway theatre about two divorced men who share an apartment. One man is very clean and organized, and the other is very messy.

- *dust*: noun: fine dirt that accumulates on and under furniture
  verb: to clean the dirt with a feather duster or cloth

- *dusty*: covered with dust

- *dust bunny*: small ball of accumulated dust

Confessions of a Messy Person
by Dorothy Nixon

1 My husband and I are a genuine Odd Couple. He is neat, and I am messy. Take our bedroom. On my husband's side, the night table is shiny-clean and **bare**, except for an alarm clock and a sleek iron lamp from Ikea. A blue laundry bag is hooked primly on the shoulder of an antique white kitchen chair. On my side, the night table is covered with dream diaries, pens, relaxation tapes, my favourite necklaces, a toothbrush, and some squished up Kleenexes. It is dusty because it is impossible to wipe such a surface. Half my summer wardrobe—skirts, pullovers, exercise outfits, and underwear—is draped over a side chair.

bare
clear, empty

2 Okay. You **get my drift**: I am not a tidy person, and as far as I recall, I have never been one. My sloppiness is a deeply ingrained personality trait. I was the only girl in the fourth grade not to get a sample of her handwriting posted on the Honour Board. The disarray in my desk regularly brought tears of frustration to my teacher's eyes. And, still, I did not change my ways. I could not. You see, my messy nature is etched into my DNA.

get my drift
understand

3 Today, I refuse to be **cowed** by it. Indeed, I prefer to rationalize my untidy ways. "I am a feminist," I say, and not a neurotic 1950s housewife who measures her self-worth by the **shine** on her kitchen linoleum. I'm not a superficial phony, afraid of what the neighbours will think. What you see is what you get, and what you get are last night's dishes in the sink, last week's newspapers on the couch, and last year's doggy chew bones on the mantelpiece.

cowed
intimidated

shine
lustre

4 I am an intellectual who would rather read a good book than Endust the furniture or Windex the windows. "Do you think the philosophers Sartre and de Beauvoir spent their days tidying up for houseguests?" I ask my husband, whose mother was a classic 1950s housewife.

5 Actually, books bore me, but I do scan magazines for facts in support of my sloppy ways. "Did you know," I continue, "that when doctors cut the connection between the right and left lobe of a patient's brain, the patient becomes compulsively neat?" I stress the word *compulsively* to make neatness sound like a disease. My husband rolls his eyes and continues to load the dishwasher.

6 "Did you know," I say, this time referring to an article in *Mother Jones Magazine*, "that every child is filled with toxins from absorbing household chemicals? The problem is cleaning fluids," I further explain in case he doesn't get it. "Imagine what all those filthy chemicals are doing to our septic tanks, to the neighbourhood ecologies, and to our planet!" But the poor man is busy picking up last week's newspapers and placing them in the recycling bin.

7 Whatever turns him on, I think. I am not prejudiced against neat people. I do not judge my friends and neighbours on their orderly kitchen shelves and dust-bunny-free bedroom floors. I do not think any less of them because *they* might feel a need to make a pristine show of it. Neatness isn't a character fault, after all. But I, Dorothy Nixon, make no apologies for who and what I am. I am a messy person.

Vocabulary and Comprehension

1 • Which word means the opposite of "clean and organized"? Circle the right answer.

   a) tidy   **(b)** messy   **c)** neat

2 • What is a *night table*? Look in Paragraph 1 for clues.

_____

3 • What is *wipe*? Look in Paragraph 1 for clues.

   a) to move   **b)** to repair   **c)** to clean with a cloth

4 • *Messiness* means "the state of being disorganized and not clean."
In Paragraph 2, find another word that means the same thing as *messiness*.

_____

5 • In Paragraphs 4 to 6, Nixon gives facts to support her messy ways. Identify four supporting points.

  ☐ Cleaning chemicals hurt the environment.
  ☐ There are many maids and servants who can clean your house.
  ☐ After brain surgery, people become compulsively neat.
  ☐ There are many books that help people to be neater.
  ☐ Cleaning liquids have dangerous chemicals that can harm children.
  ☐ She is an intellectual, and famous intellectuals never worried about cleaning the house.

Identify if the following statements are true (T) or false (F). If the sentence is false, write a true sentence under it.

6 • Dorothy Nixon did not write neatly when she was in school............ T   F

_____

➡

7• Dorothy Nixon likes reading books more than magazines. .... T   F

_____

8• Dorothy Nixon's husband cleans the dishes and removes the old
newspapers. .... T   F

_____

Verb Hunt

9• Look in Paragraph 1. The first two sentences contain three forms of the
verb *be*. What are they? Write the three subjects and verbs.

_____   _____   _____

10• In Paragraph 5, Nixon writes, "My husband rolls his eyes and continues to
load the dishwasher." Why do the verbs *rolls* and *continues* end in *-s*?

_____

Speaking ·· Good and Bad Habits

Interview another student. Look at the list below, and indicate which habits
your partner has or doesn't have.

DO YOU DO THE FOLLOWING ON A REGULAR BASIS?					
BAD HABITS	YES	NO	**BEDROOM/SLEEP HABITS**	YES	NO
bite your nails	X		sleep late	X	
drink too much alcohol	X		read in bed	X	X
break promises	X	X	make your bed	X	
tease people	X		tidy your bedroom	X	
smoke	X		put away clothes	X	
watch too much TV		X	have a daily nap (siesta)		X
drive too fast		X	sleep eight hours or more each night		X
CLEANLINESS HABITS	YES	NO	**EXPRESSIVE HABITS**	YES	NO
floss your teeth	X		lose your temper easily	X	
wash your own dishes		X	**spend*** time alone		X
clean your bathtub after using it	X		laugh easily	X	
put the lid on the toothpaste		X	cry easily		X
clean your fingernails		X	sing in the shower	X	
clean your desk		X	doodle (make drawings while you are thinking or listening)	X	

*Note: the word *spend* means "to pass time" in this context.

Writing Activity

Write a paragraph about your partner's habits. Describe what your partner generally does and doesn't do.

> **Tip** Grammar
>
> **Third-Person Singular**
>
> When you describe another person's habits, remember to put an -s or -es at the end of each verb. Add *does not* to negative forms.
>
> She **bites** her nails when she feels nervous.
>
> He **does** **not** **make** his bed because he is lazy.

When you finish, make sure that your paragraph is well structured. You can refer to the paragraph checklist on the inside back cover.

Watching ·· George and Rosemary

German-born development expert Erik Erikson developed a theory about life stages. He believed that humans go through eight life stages, and at each stage, people are faced with a central conflict that they must overcome. For instance, adolescents must choose from a variety of goals and values to create an identity.

According to Erikson, one of the central tasks in adulthood is to commit oneself to another person in an intimate relationship. In the next video, a man named George has a secret passion for the lady who lives across the street.

Pre-Watching Vocabulary

Look at the following expressions. Write the letter of the correct picture in the space.

1 • knock on the door _____

2 • pick up the phone _____

3 • hang up the phone _____

4 • play checkers _____

   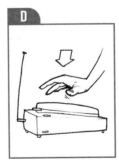

Watching Comprehension

For questions 1, 2, 3, and 6, circle the letter of the right answer.

1 • At the beginning of the video, what is George's house number?

   a) 14   **b)** 40   **c)** 42

2 • On rainy days, what does George *not* do?

   a) Sit on his porch and watch people.   **c)** Play checkers with his cat.

   b) Put ships in jars.   **d)** Watch TV and eat.

3 • What is Rosemary's last name?

   a) Harris   **b)** Edgecomb   **c)** Basil

4 • George tries to phone Rosemary. What happens when she picks up the phone?

_____

5 • What is George's last name? _____

6 • What type of cookies does the little girl try to sell to George?

   a) ginger   **b)** oatmeal   **c)** chocolate chip

7 • What happens when George finally knocks on Rosemary's door?

_____

8 • Why does Rosemary have binoculars near her window?

_____

9 • What lesson can we learn from this story?

_____

To develop your listening skills, visit the companion website.

Reading

Reading 1.3

Martin Neufeld is a classically trained actor from the London Academy of Music and Dramatic Arts. He has appeared in numerous feature films and television series. At the turn of the millennium, a personal crisis brought on a life change. Today, Neufeld is the Hugger Busker, a public hugger, and he has published a book about his experiences called *Hugging Life*. (See www.hugginglife.com.) As you read, don't stop at unfamiliar words. Try to understand the main ideas.

Pre-Reading Vocabulary

Before reading the essay, review the following definitions.

- *busker*:   street performer, artist, or musician
- *to hug*:   to hold someone in your arms
- *livelihood*: occupation that pays for living expenses
- *to act*:   to perform for an audience

The Hugger Busker
An interview with Martin Neufeld

1 *How would you describe your childhood personality?*

2 I was solitary and sensitive. I liked being the centre of attention, yet in the company of others I became **shy** and reserved. Like most kids, I had a desire to fit in and be appreciated.

shy
timid

3 *What made you choose acting as a professional career?*

4 I remember very clearly the moment I decided to be an actor. It was a week before my tenth birthday, and my parents brought me to see a play by the Montreal Children's Theatre. During the intermission, my father asked me what I wanted for my birthday. I pointed to the theatre stage and said, "I want to act in a play like those other children." Soon after, I was in drama classes with those same children, and three months later I had my first small role in a production of *Hansel and Gretel*.

5 My interest in acting continued to my adulthood. After graduating from the Dawson College Theatre Department, I was offered the lead role in a miniseries called *The Tin Flute*. This film launched my career, and for the next twenty years I travelled around the world working on numerous film, television, and theatre projects. Acting had become my life and my livelihood.

6 *Was acting a rewarding occupation?*

7 The profession was very good to me. I travelled to many fascinating places, such as the Arctic Circle, Paris, London, New York, and Bangkok. I studied theatre in London, and in Paris I trained under the grand theatre master Jacques Lecoq. To get paid to act is wonderful, though it is a lot of hard work.

8 The life of an actor is feast or famine. You never know when your next job or paycheque will come. You can have no work for a year and then get so much work that you have to turn down projects. You need a strong character, persistence, and resilience to succeed in show business.

9 In spite of the instability of this business, I just loved being on stage in front of an audience or in front of the camera. I felt truly vibrant and alive. It was exciting and creatively liberating for me to portray a character who had a different personality and lived in a different world. It was like being a little boy again and going on another wonderful adventure.

10 I felt that it was possible through my acting to bring pleasure and positive change to the lives of those who watched me perform. Yet as I got older, the roles offered to me changed from being **light-hearted** and **quirky** to dark and disturbing. I found that I was really good at playing angry and dangerous men even though I was really a kind and compassionate person. Because I excelled at those portrayals, I became typecast as the innocent-looking bad guy.

light-hearted
optimistic

quirky
unusual; eccentric

11 It is difficult when directors and producers identify you as a particular type of character—the secretive neighbour or the grouchy detective or the charming murderer or the lovesick boyfriend—and then you are stuck

playing the same kind of role over and over, even if you can be brilliant at others. An example of this is when I played Snake, a heroin addict, in the award-winning film *H*. I created a very realistic portrayal of a junkie. And in the Christmas television movie *Silent Night*, I played a hard-nosed, cruel German officer. So for years, producers offered me the same kind of roles. Typecasting is creative death for any actor.

>>> Neufeld in a scene from *Silent Night*.

12 The moods that I created for these dark roles were harder to **deal with** as the years went by. My discomfort with the negativity that I was portraying began to affect me on a personal level. I craved to play valiant, kind, or even funny characters. Yet I was becoming just like the unhappy, confused, and angry men that I portrayed. My dream of being a source of joy and inspiration for others was getting lost. It was then that I decided to step back and re-evaluate my profession and my life.

deal with
manage

13 *Why did you change your focus from acting to hugging? What brought that on?*

14 In June 2004, I decided to go back to my roots as a physical theatre actor and explore street performance. I went to Place Jacques-Cartier, a public square in Old Montreal with many shops, restaurants, and tourists. That is where one can find many of the best street performers. Guy Laliberté, the founder of Cirque du Soleil, started his career as a street performer there.

15 I created a series of strange and amusing improvisations based on a character that I had developed; a very elegant, charming, and cheerful clown without the red nose. I grabbed an old leather suitcase and an umbrella, put on my green felt hat, and went to the square to entertain. It was hard for me at first to find the right spot and then get a crowd to stop, watch, and pay.

16 I was not very good at it. In fact, the first few days I did not even have the courage to perform. Yet I persisted, and within a week I was improvising with the best of them. Every day I would write a thoughtful **saying** on one of the little chalkboards leaning on my suitcase. Then one day, I was trying to think of something meaningful to write when I remembered seeing a café advertise its special of the day. So I wrote "Special of the Day" on my board.

saying
expression

17 But what did I have to offer that is special? Then I had an idea. I love hugging my family and friends, so why not write "Free Hugs!" I did not stop to think about the consequences of my words or actions. I simply stood tall and absolutely still on a tiny Persian rug, and I opened my arms invitingly to the world at large.

Source: Photo by François Miron from *Hugging Life*—a book by Martin Neufeld.

18 *How did people react to you?*

19 Many people stopped, mesmerized by my stillness. Then they would read my sign, smile, and some would approach shyly for a hug. Some people thought I was weird, but even those who did not hug me looked a little more **cheerful**. With each hug I shared, my heart became more and more open, and the hugs became infused with loving kindness and comfort.

cheerful
happy

20 About 75,000 hugs later, I am still sharing my **heartfelt** art in public squares. Sometimes someone who is very sad or upset will come to see me for a comforting hug, and I am very honoured when a stranger chooses me as a source of reassurance. I am happy to bring some caring and comfort to the world one hug at a time.

heartfelt
sincere

Comprehension

1 • When did Martin Neufeld realize that he wanted to be an actor?

_____

2 • What does Neufeld like about being an actor?

a) He can travel to many different places.

b) He enjoys playing characters who have different personalities.

c) He loves being in front of a camera or on stage.

d) All of the answers.

3 • What are some disadvantages of being an actor? Think of two things.

_____

4 • In Paragraph 10, Neufeld says that he was typecast. What does he mean?

_____

5 • Why was Neufeld typecast as an angry and dangerous character?

_____

6 • Why did Neufeld change his focus from film acting to street theatre? What was the main reason?

a) He did not want to act anymore. He was bored with television and film work.

b) He was tired of playing negative and angry characters, and it was affecting his personal life.

c) He had no more money.

7 • What does Neufeld do during his street performances?

_____

Visit the companion website to view clips from Martin Neufeld's many film and television productions.

8 • What did Neufeld learn about himself during his years as an actor?

Writing Topics

To review some of the vocabulary studied in this chapter, visit the companion website.

Compose a text about one of the following topics.

1 • Describe what Martin Neufeld does. Explain how a hugger busker is useful in our world.

2 • Poet Sidney Madwed once said, "If you want to be truly successful, invest in yourself." Write about things you are doing to invest in yourself. What are you doing to give yourself a better life?

>> *Stress is an ignorant state. It believes that everything is an emergency. Nothing is that important.* >>

Nathalie Goldberg

Balancing Act

How much stress do you have in your life? Do you work and study? Do you have time to relax? This chapter looks at busy lives.

 **Warm Up** ·· Survey

Get into a team with three or four other students and find out about their work and study habits.

Name of student	Leisure-time activities	Type of part-time job (If no job, explain why)	Hours per week of part-time work	Hours per week of homework	Hours per night of sleep (average)

Brainstorm with team members. List two benefits and two disadvantages of having a part-time job while studying.

BENEFITS OF A PART-TIME JOB	DISADVANTAGES OF A PART-TIME JOB
_____	_____
_____	_____

Reading

Reading Strategy

To practise writing about routines, visit the companion website.

Using Context Clues

You can understand the meaning of many words and expressions by looking at the word in its context. To guess the meaning of a new word, you can try the following strategies.

1• **Determine the part of speech.**
   Is the word a noun? Is it a verb? Is it an adjective? Sometimes it is easier to understand a word if you know what part of speech the word is.

2• **Look at the parts of the word.**
   Identify prefixes and suffixes to help you find the meaning of a word. For example, some common prefixes meaning "not" include *un-* (*unhappy*), *il-* (*illegal*), *dis-* (*dissatisfied*), and *im-* (*immoral*).

3• **Look at surrounding words.**
   Other words in a sentence can help define the key word.

4• **Look for a synonym (a word that means the same thing) or antonym (word that means the opposite).**

5• **Look at surrounding sentences.**
   Look at the sentences and paragraphs surrounding the word for clues to its meaning.

Reading Exercise

One word in each sentence is in italics. Answer the questions that follow to determine the meaning of the word.

Example: The extremely **shy** student refused to raise her hand. She was too scared to speak in front of the other students.

- Part of speech: ____*adjective*____ (The word describes the type of student, so *shy* must be an adjective.)

- Meaning: ____*timid*____

- Clue: ____*"scared to speak"*____

1• I need some extra **cash** because it costs a lot to repair my car.

   Part of speech: _____

Meaning: _____

Clue: _____

2 • Mr. and Mrs. Perez are extremely excited because their business
is booming! They have more customers every day!

Part of speech: _____

Meaning: _____

Clue: _____

3 • Anne is eating a plate of **raw** carrots and broccoli. She never cooks
her vegetables because the cooking process removes too many
nutrients.

Part of speech: _____

Meaning: _____

Clue: _____

4 • As she walked, Kelly **shifted** her heavy books from one arm to the other.

Part of speech: _____

Meaning: _____

Clue: _____

5 • Philippe is an **unreliable** worker. He is often late, and he loses the keys.

Part of speech: _____

Meaning: _____

Clue: _____

Reading 2.1

In the following text, Nanci Hellmich looks at the dangers of sleep deprivation.
On the line next to each highlighted word, write a short definition or
translation. Use context clues to guess the meaning of each word.

Too Busy to Sleep
by Nanci Hellmich
USA Today

Write definition

1   Molly Melamed, seventeen, a high school junior in Farmington Hills,
Michigan, crawls out of bed at 5:45 every morning and **dashes** to   *runs*
school for her 7:20 a.m. class. After school, she goes to student council
meetings, pompom practice, guitar lessons, or one of two jobs:
waitressing or teaching horseback riding lessons.

2   She comes home to lots of homework and phone calls with friends.
She's lucky if she gets into bed at 11 p.m. "I'm out cold," she says.
Melamed knows **lack** of sleep is taking a toll. "I'm always tired.   _____

Sometimes my alarm clock will go off and I sleep right through it, or I'll hear it and go back to sleep because I think it's a dream."

3 She didn't realize how dangerous sleep deprivation was until a friend fell asleep at the wheel and was killed in a car crash. At school, they discuss the **hazards** of drinking and driving, but not driving while sleepy, she says. "Until he died, no one understood how dangerous it was not to get your sleep."

4 A new scientific study shows that on average, teenagers are getting about two hours less sleep a night than they need, putting them at risk for automobile accidents, falling asleep in class, and general moodiness. A poll from the National Sleep Foundation confirms that teens are staying up too late and waking up too early.

5 Adolescent sleep researcher Mary Carskadon says that, for optimal functioning, teens need nine hours and fifteen minutes of sleep a night. Sleep deprivation is a serious matter for teens. Of the estimated 100,000 car crashes a year linked to **sleepy** driving, almost half involve drivers aged fifteen to twenty-four, according to the U.S. Department of Transportation's National Highway Traffic Safety Administration.

6 Neurologist Mark Mahowald, director of the Minnesota Regional Sleep Disorders Center, believes the number of teen car crashes from falling asleep at the wheel is even higher than reported because "sleepiness doesn't show up on the autopsy. I'm tired of reading about dead teenagers killed at the prime of their lives due to falling asleep driving."

7 Experts, parents, and teachers are troubled by this sleep deprivation among adolescents for other reasons too. Students who are tired are more likely to **doze off** in class and are less able to concentrate, learn, and solve problems. The irony is that many students are staying up late to study so they can get into good colleges.

8 "Teens need more sleep," Mahowald says. But teens live in a society that doesn't value sleep, he says. Mahowald notes, "We want our kids to do more, more, more." He says that if you need an alarm clock to wake up in the morning, you're sleep-deprived.

9 When adolescents don't get as much sleep as they need, it changes their outlook on life, Carskadon says. "Kids walk around **under a grey cloud**. Things that are happy and pleasant seem less so. And things that are sad and unpleasant seem more so."

10 Pediatrician Ronald Dahl says teens, like adults, become more emotional when they are sleep-deprived. If something strikes them as funny, they may get silly and **giggly**. If something is sad, they are more likely to cry. And if they are frustrated or angry, they have a harder time controlling their emotions, he says. Parents and teens should try to cut back on the activities so sleep isn't squeezed out, experts say. When teens do get enough sleep, Carskadon says, "they feel an incredible mental clarity."

Comprehension

1 • Why doesn't Molly Melamed sleep enough? _____

_____

2 • What three problems can sleep deprivation cause? _____

_____

3 • According to Mary Carskadon, how much sleep should a teen get each night?

_____

4 • What percentage of sleep-related car crashes are caused by teenagers?
Circle the right answer.

   a) almost 25%   **b)** almost 50%   **c)** almost 80%

5 • According to Mark Mahowald, how can people discover if they are sleep-deprived? (See Paragraph 8 for ideas.)

_____

6 • What can parents and teens do to minimize sleep deprivation? (See Paragraph 10 and restate the idea in your own words.)

_____

_____

7 • What is this text about? Circle the appropriate answer.

   a) Many teenagers are not getting enough sleep, and it can cause serious problems.

   b) Molly Melamed does not get enough sleep.

   c) Teenagers have too many activities.

   d) People should sleep for at least nine hours each night.

Dicussion

1 • Do you get enough sleep? Do you need an alarm clock to wake you up?

2 • Would it be possible for you to get nine hours of sleep each night? Why or why not?

3 • Do you think this text exaggerates the importance of sleep? Explain.

Listening

Pronunciation

Part 1: Pronounce Verbs Ending in -s or -es

Pronounce each pair of words after the speaker. Pay attention to the pronunciation of the letter *s* at the end of the words. You will say each verb twice.   ➡

Example: *push – pushes*

1. go – goes	6. wish – wishes	11. laugh – laughs
2. watch – watches	7. march – marches	12. ask – asks
3. walk – walks	8. believe – believes	13. live – lives
4. kiss – kisses	9. wash – washes	14. fix – fixes
5. hope – hopes	10. sleep – sleeps	15. teach – teaches

Part 2: Pronounce Sentences

Pronounce the following sentences after the speaker. You will say each sentence twice. Remember to pronounce the final *s* on words.

1. Rebecca likes to read books.
2. Jason has many friends.
3. Julie sometimes uses the Internet.
4. My sister teaches in a high school.
5. Those girls often play football.
6. That nurse finishes work at five o'clock.
7. My lawyer needs more clients.
8. My father watches a lot of TV.
9. He rarely listens to the radio.
10. Carol never washes the dishes.

Listening The Sleep Clinic

Many clinics now focus on sleep disorders. The following discussion takes place between a sleep specialist and her patient.

Pre-Listening Vocabulary

Before you listen, verify that you understand the following terms. If you don't understand a term, then check the word in your dictionary or ask your teacher.

pills	addictive	supper	meal	midnight

Listening Comprehension

Listen to the dialogue between a patient and his doctor, and then answer the questions that follow.

1 • What is Martin's major problem? _____

2 • Does Martin have a nap each afternoon? .... ☐Yes ☐No

3 • How many hours of sleep does Martin get each night, generally? _____

4 • At what time does Martin drink his last coffee of the day? _____

5 • When does Martin generally eat supper? _____

6 • Martin usually has a large snack at about 10 p.m. at night. What type of food does Martin eat for his late-day snack? _____

Are the following statements true or false? Circle T for "true" or F for "false."

7 • Martin lives alone. ....T   F

8 • Martin exercises every day. ....T   F

9 • Martin usually eats supper in a restaurant. ....T   F

10 • Martin generally falls asleep around midnight. ....T   F

11 • The doctor likes to prescribe sleeping pills for her patients..............T   F

12 • The doctor gives Martin three pieces of advice. What is her advice? (Circle three answers).

<table>
<tr><td>a) eat more fruits and vegetables</td><td>e) go for a walk after supper</td></tr>
<tr><td>b) stop drinking Coke at night</td><td>f) read before you go to bed</td></tr>
<tr><td>c) stop drinking coffee</td><td>g) take a nap in the afternoon</td></tr>
<tr><td>d) try some sleeping pills</td><td>h) eat less food before you go to bed</td></tr>
</table>

Reading

Reading 2.2

The following diary entry was written by Naomi Louder, a college student and part-time waitress. Read about her experiences.

Juggling Acts: A Day in the Life
by Naomi Louder

1 **6:45 a.m.** The alarm sounds like an ambulance that is charging through my bedroom. I hit the snooze button. For a few seconds I lie awake, traumatized. It is exam week. I worry about the essay I handed in yesterday. I worry about today's shift. I wonder when I will have time to study. I worry about money. I am sure that nobody will tip me at the restaurant because I'll be so tired that I'll spill coffee on customers and I'll forget orders. Then my boss will fire me. If I am going to get fired anyway, I might as well sleep in. I fall asleep.

2 **6:54 a.m.** The alarm rings again. Half asleep, I shut it off.

3 **7:00 a.m.** A shower wakes me up into a state of full awareness of how much I hate mornings. I go back into the bedroom and rummage for work clothes. I did laundry yesterday, but I didn't put it away. Half the pile of clothing has slid off the dresser onto the floor. I quickly pull on my uniform, and I stuff jeans and a shirt into my bag. Later today, I don't want to go the library smelling like a day-old lunch.

4 **8:00 a.m.** I arrive at work. Automatic pilot kicks in, and I serve well. My tips are better than usual. My co-workers invite me to a birthday party at a terrace tonight. I agree to come if I can get enough studying done this afternoon.

5 **4:00 p.m.** My shift is over. I change into my street clothes. I realize that I forgot to pack the book and the notes I need. I consider going home to get them, and a picture creeps into my consciousness: my bedroom with curtains closed, the fan on, and cool sheets. It's too dangerous to go there.

6 **4:30 p.m.** The heat and close proximity of other passengers on this bus is quickly making my good mood and my clean shirt a memory.

7 **5:00 p.m.** I enter the library, and I want to hug the person who invented air conditioning. It is quiet and cool here, and it should be easy to concentrate.

8 **5:30 p.m.** Far away, I hear a voice: "Miss. Miss. Miss. I'm sorry miss. Miss. MISS. You can't sleep in the library, miss." A security guard is standing over me.

9 "I'm studying," I mumble indignantly. He walks away, looking skeptical.

10 **8:30 p.m.** I am well ahead in my studying, so I decide to treat myself to cheap sushi. I leave the library and head to a nearby restaurant. While I am waiting for my order, my cellphone rings for the first time all day. Work and school take up so much time that my friends rarely call me. They know that I'm always too busy to hang out. It's my roommate on the phone. "The stove doesn't work," she tells me. "I called the gas company and they say you didn't pay the bill." I promise to call the gas company. My sushi arrives but my appetite is gone.

11 Using my cellphone again, I call the gas company. They tell me that I'm going to have to pay a $200 reconnection fee, plus a $60 technician fee, plus my bill, which is $78.

12 **9:30 p.m.** Frustrated, wanting to forget my life, I decide to go to that party on the terrace with my workmates. I am oddly re-energized as I spend the next few hours laughing, chatting, and drinking icy beverages.

13 **3:00 a.m.** At home, I drink a litre of water and set my alarm for 6:45 as usual. Tomorrow I will definitely get fired. During my afternoon exam, I will forget everything that I studied. I lie awake, worried about getting up in three hours.

14 **6:45 a.m.** The alarm sounds like an ambulance that is charging through my bedroom.

Vocabulary •• Using Context Clues

Define the following terms using clues from the text.

Example: Define *fire* (Paragraph 1). _to force out of a job_

1 • In Paragraph 1, what is the meaning of *tip*? _____

2 • Find a word in Paragraph 3 that means "search for." _____

3 • In Paragraph 3, what is a *dresser*?

   a) a person who helps you put on your clothing

   b) a type of clothing

   c) a piece of furniture where you can keep clean clothing

4 • In Paragraph 4, what is the meaning of *kicks in*? _____

5 • In Paragraph 7, what is the meaning of *hug*?

   a) hit   **b)** embrace   **c)** ignore

6 • In Paragraph 10, what is a *roommate*? _____

7 • Find a two-word expression in Paragraph 10 that means "to spend time together." _____

Comprehension

Identify if the following statements are true (T) or false (F). Circle the right answer.

8 • In the early morning, an ambulance drives by Naomi's window. ....T   F

9 • At her restaurant job, Naomi gets very bad tips on this day. ....T   F

10 • Naomi wears a uniform at work. ....T   F

11 • After her shift at the restaurant, Naomi goes home to get her books. ....T   F

12 • Naomi falls asleep in the library. ....T   F

13 • Who forgot to pay the gas bill?

   a) Naomi   **b)** Naomi's roommate

Verb Hunt

14 • Look at the last sentence in the essay (Paragraph 14). Underline the first verb and circle the subject. Why does the verb end in *s*?

_____

15 • What are the complete forms of the following contractions?

   I'm _____   I'll _____   don't _____

To perfect your reading skills, visit the companion website.

Discussion

1 • Naomi is a waitress. Should servers always get tips? Why or why not?

2 • What other workers receive tips? List some.

Speaking ·· Telling the Time / Asking Lifestyle Questions

Part 1: Telling the Time

Do you know how to tell the time in English? When you schedule meetings or appointments, the ability to understand and say the time correctly is extremely important.

Review the following examples. Notice that there are at least two ways to say the time.

`12:00`	It is twelve o'clock.	It is noon.	It is midnight.
`3:15`	It is three fifteen.	It is a quarter past three.	
`5:30`	It is five thirty.	It is half past five.	
`9:45`	It is nine forty-five.	It is a quarter to ten.	

Work with a partner, and take turns reading the times indicated below. Say each time in two different ways.

Example: 12:20   It is twelve twenty.   It is twenty after twelve.

1 • 2:50   3 • 6:05   5 • 3:20   7 • 7:10   9 • 12:00

2 • 9:45   4 • 1:10   6 • 3:40   8 • 6:50   10 • 5:30

Telling Time
Only use *o'clock* when it is exactly one o'clock, two o'clock, three o'clock, and so on.
You cannot say "two fifteen o'clock."

Part 2: Asking Lifestyle Questions

Work with a partner and do the following:

• Add an auxiliary to each question. Insert *is*, *am*, *are*, *do*, or *does*.

• Write your partner's answers in the blanks.

Example: Where _____*do*_____ you work?

Answer: _____*at a service station*_____

Partner's name: _____

1 • Who _____ you live with?

Answer: _____

2 • _____ you pay rent each month?

Answer: (Explain why or why not.) _____

_____

3. What _____ your biggest expense each month?

Answer: _____

4. What _____ your hobbies?

Answer: _____

5. What time _____ you go to bed on weekends?

Answer: _____

6. When _____ your alarm clock ring each weekday morning?

Answer: _____

7. What time of the day _____ the most stressful for you?

Answer: (Describe it.) _____

_____

_____

8. Where _____ you go to relax?

Answer: _____

9. What _____ you do on weekends?

Answer: _____

10. Which one _____ you prefer: the city or the countryside?

Answer: (Explain why.) _____

_____

_____

Writing Activity

Write a paragraph about your partner. Describe his or her lifestyle.

 Grammar

Life vs. *Live*

Notice the difference between *life* and *live*.

> *Life* (noun): Humans have one **life**.
> Plural form: A myth states that cats have nine **lives**.
>
> *To live* (verb): We **live** in Montreal.
> Third-person singular form: She **lives** in Montreal.
>
> *Live* (adjective): We sometimes go to clubs and listen to **live** music.
> (There is no plural form for adjectives.)

To develop your listening skills, visit the companion website.

Reading

Reading 2.3

Eugene Henry spent nine months as a telephone salesman. In the following essay, Henry describes his experience. When you see unfamiliar words, try to guess their meanings by using context clues.

I, Telemarketer
by Eugene Henry

1   It's a familiar experience: The phone rings, and you find yourself listening to a telemarketer. Depending on your resolve, you might end the unwanted communication in ten or twenty seconds—maybe as long as a minute for the weak-willed or those with especially good manners. Either way, the call usually comes as an annoying interruption in your busy life. However, there's a whole world on the other end of your phone cord, a world in which telemarketing is not one of life's interruptions, but life itself. In late 2003, I became part of that world when I became a telemarketer.

2   Montreal is North America's call-centre capital, and despite the impression one gets from investigative news reports, many are perfectly respectable employers. Some even recruit at career fairs—which is where, fresh out of university, I came across a promising-looking outfit that offered me a modest signing bonus and a respectable salary. The firm was part of a large, publicly traded telemarketing company based in the United States, with call centres in twenty-six countries. The size was comforting. It meant I wouldn't have to worry about working at the sort of fly-by-night operation that ends up being **raided** by the RCMP.

raided
entered and searched

3   During my training, I learned more than I ever wanted to know about cable television packages. Our goal was to sell premium movie channels to existing cable customers, and this would become my professional mission over the next few months.

4   Workers at a call centre are divided into a day shift and a night shift, and everyone works from a desk with a computer and a phone in a large, colourless room. The work isn't pleasant, and the days go by slowly.

5   The pressure to sell is intense. Telemarketers who don't make quota tend to disappear. Someone you've worked with for a while and talked with on breaks or at lunch will one day simply stop showing up. They are usually fired, though sometimes they quit.

6   I almost lost my own job in November, shortly after I started. There was an incentive prize of fifty dollars for the employee with the best "conversion"—the ratio of sales to calls—which is a lot of money for a telemarketer. I wasn't a bad salesman, mainly because I didn't push. (A casual manner on the phone works better than someone who sounds desperate or aggressive.) But to win the fifty dollars, I knew I needed to cheat. So

28

I put down people who rejected my pitch as wrong numbers, which meant they would be kept out of my conversion ratio, artificially boosting it. Unfortunately, a "quality assurance monitor"—the big brothers of the call centre—discovered my ruse. It was **grounds** for immediate dismissal, but my sales were decent so they kept me on.

grounds
reason or justification

7 Others weren't so lucky. Over our Christmas break, almost all of my colleagues were laid off. We were all supposed to return from our Christmas break on January 5. Instead, Human Resources called most of us on January 4 to instruct us not to come in the next day.

8 I felt guilty about surviving the **purge**. Most telemarketers are hard-luck cases who live on the margins of the job market. In other words, the people who lost their jobs needed the work more than I did. I didn't have a family to feed—like my single-mother colleague who had no way to pay the bills that had piled up over the holidays.

purge
elimination of employees

9 As March and April wore on, I fell in love with one of the "big brothers." Kelly was a twenty-six-year-old graphic designer. We had a lot to talk about—mostly how she'd rather be designing things and I'd rather be writing things.

10 I found that being in a secret relationship with the person monitoring your calls helps make telemarketing easier. I had carte blanche to slack off. I even started writing at my desk between calls. Kelly told me there was nothing to worry about, as long as I made enough sales to pass under the radar of her managers. It was a high-stakes sacrifice on her part: She could have lost her job if anyone found out she was cutting someone slack on the floor.

11 Despite Kelly's help, May, which would become my last full month on the job, was a difficult one. The cable company was trying to move everyone to digital, and so we were schooled on the superiority of digital television technology. The job meant calling **retired** people who had no idea what digital was. Notwithstanding their ignorance, it was our job to "increase their bill a few dollars" so they could enjoy digital splendour.

retired
older and no longer working

12 One guy on the floor found an effective strategy. Salman, a Pakistani Muslim, had recently arrived in Montreal by way of Florida. His strategy for selling digital was to find "specialty channels" that he knew would catch old people's interest. There were a few channels that focus on Christian programming, and Sal found it amusing that he, of all people, had so much success pitching them to pensioners. "It's easy," he told me. "All you have to do is sell Jesus. Jesus sells himself."

13 By the end of May, I'd been on the job nine months, and I'd had enough. I asked Human Resources how to quit. They told me to write a notice and give it to my team manager. When I actually did this, everyone seemed surprised. Apparently, I'm among the small minority of telemarketers who actually give two weeks' notice. Consistent with the disposable employment ethos that governs the profession, many simply stop showing up.

14 Nine months may not seem like a long time, but I think I learned more during that period than I did during four years of university. Certainly, I learned to be more respectful when the phone rings and I hear a stranger's voice.

15 The next time you talk to a telemarketer, think about a polite "no thanks" instead of the all-too-common expletive or hang-up. Sometimes that's enough to get a telemarketer through the day with at least a half-smile on his or her face.

Vocabulary

1 • What is a *telemarketer*? _____

2 • What is the meaning of *recruit* in Paragraph 2?
   a) to feel happy   **b)** to finish   **c)** to look for employees

3 • Find a word in Paragraph 6 that means "increasing; making larger."

   _____

4 • What is a *pitch* in Paragraph 6?
   a) money   **b)** a sales speech   **c)** friend

5 • What is the meaning of *slack off* in Paragraph 10?

   _____

Comprehension

6 • What did Henry sell?
   a) televisions   **b)** cellphones   **c)** cable television packages

7 • What is not true about Henry's sales technique?
   a) He pushes customers and is very forceful.
   b) He is casual and doesn't push.

8 • In Paragraph 8, why does Henry feel bad about keeping his job?
   a) He did not deserve to keep it because he was a bad worker.
   b) Some people who lost their jobs needed the work more than Henry did.
   c) His girlfriend was his manager.

9 • When Henry's manager became his girlfriend, how did it affect his work?

   _____

10 • Henry says that he learned more at his job "than during four years of university." Think of some positive and negative lessons that he learned.

   _____

   _____

   _____

   _____

Dicussion

1 • How do you respond when a telemarketer calls?

2 • Should telemarketing be illegal? Why or why not?

3 • What unethical actions does Henry do during his telemarketing job?

Watching •• No Free Time

Many people say that they are too busy. Working mothers complain that they don't have time with the children and students complain that they have no free time. Are people in our society really suffering from a lack of free time? Watch the next video and find out.

Pre-Watching Vocabulary

Before watching the video, ensure that you understand the following words. Write the letter of the correct definition in the blank space.

TERM		DEFINITION
1. free time	_____	a. a journal where people write down private thoughts
2. diary	_____	b. something that is not logical
3. rush	_____	c. increase
4. fewer	_____	d. time to do leisure activities
5. nonsense	_____	e. move quickly
6. gain	_____	f. a smaller number

Watching for Main Ideas

Watch the video and identify the main ideas.

1 • Stephen Moore is an economist. What is his opinion about free time?

    a) People had more free time in the past.

    b) People have more free time today.

2 • In the interviews, what do most ordinary people believe about free time?

    a) They believe that they are too busy and have almost no free time.

    b) They believe that they have more free time than people had in the past.

3 • Using your own words, describe the main idea of the video segment.

_____

_____

_____

Watching for Details

Watch the video again. Listen for specific details. Decide if the following statements are true (T) or false (F).

4 • Sherry Kowalowski has two children. .... T   F

5 • Since 1965, we have gained about one more hour
of free time per day. .... T   F

6 • Sherry Kowalski rarely exercices. .... T   F

7 • These days, what is the most popular free-time activity?

   a) watching TV   **b)** playing sports   **c)** cleaning the house

8 • Fifty years ago, how much time per week did the average woman spend washing clothing?

   a) ten hours   **b)** sixty to seventy hours   **c)** one hundred hours

9 • What is the name of Stephen Moore's book?

   a) *No Free Time*

   b) *What Can We Do?*

   c) *It's Getting Better All the Time*

10 • Why were people so much busier in the past?

   _____

   _____

   _____

Speaking ·· A Peaceful Place

Where do you go when you feel stressed and you just want to relax? Think about a place that is very important to you. It could be a part of your home such as your bedroom, basement, or backyard. It could be a public place such as a park, restaurant, coffee shop, library, or dance club. It could also be a place where you go on vacation.

Do the following:

1 • Describe how your special place looks.

2 • Describe some things that you generally do in that place.

3 • Explain why that place is important to you.

4 • Bring along something visual. You can bring a photograph or drawing of the place, or bring a special object that belongs to that place.

Classmates will ask you some questions about your peaceful place.

Presentation

You can use notes or cue cards with the main words. Do not read! Put a maximum of fifteen words on your cue cards.

Practise your presentation. Time yourself. You must speak for two to three minutes.

Writing Topics

Write about one of the following topics. When you finish writing, refer to the relevant checklist on the inside back cover.

1 • Describe your lifestyle. Is your lifestyle very stressful? How much sleep do you get? What do you do to relax?

2 • Describe the lifestyle of a family member. When does that person get up? Does he or she need an alarm to wake up? Does he or she work a lot? When does that person relax? (Remember to put -*s* or -*es* on verbs when the subject is third-person singular.)

3 • Write a journal about a day in your life. Make your journal similar in structure to Reading 2.2.

To review some of the vocabulary studied in this chapter, visit the companion website.

4 • Write an essay about part-time jobs. In one paragraph, describe the advantages of having a part-time job while you are going to college. In another paragraph, describe the disadvantages of doing part-time work.

5 • In "I, Telemarketer," the author had a workplace romance. What are some advantages and disadvantages of dating a co-worker?

6 • Should waiters or other service workers always receive tips? Why or why not? Support your ideas with personal anecdotes.

Trends

•• *A fashion is nothing but an induced epidemic.* ••

George Bernard Shaw

What fads and fashions have you followed? In this chapter, you will read about some past and present fads.

Warm Up •• Physical Descriptions

Pair Work •• Describe the Photo

Find a partner.

• One of you will look at the photo below.

• The other will look at the photo on page 48.

• There are eight differences in the photos. Describe your photo and ask questions to find the differences. Do not cheat and look at the other photo!

• Working with your partner, write down the differences on a separate piece of paper. Make complete sentences. When you finish, check if your verbs are correct.

Example: In photo A, the girl with long brown hair is not serious. She is smiling.

Using -ing Verbs

When you describe something that is happening right now, use the present progressive. Use *be* plus the *-ing* verb form.

> He **is wearing** a black shirt. They **are not eating**.

In the question form, simply place *be* before the subject.

> What **is** he **wearing**?

The following terms are used to describe a person's physical appearance. Review the terms.

FACE		HAIR AND BODY ART		CLOTHING AND PATTERNS	
dimple	bald (no hair)	brunette	*Clothing*	*Patterns*
hooked nose	bangs	grey	belt	dots
mole	braids	red	coat	flowers
pimple	curly		dress	plaid
scar	dyed	*Facial Hair:*	glasses	stripes
turned-up nose	frizzy	beard	pants	
wrinkles	long	goatee	scarf	*Parts of*
	short	moustache	shirt	*clothing:*
Eye Colour:	shoulder-length	sideburns	shorts	button
blue	straight	whiskers	skirt	collar
brown	streaked		socks	sleeve
green	wavy	*Body Art:*	sweater	zipper
hazel		eyebrow ring	T-shirt	
	Hair Colour:	pierced ears	tank top	
	black	pierced nose	tie	
	blond	tattoo	underwear	

To work on your writing skills, visit the companion website.

 **Reading**

Reading **Strategy**

Identifying Cognates (Word Twins)

Many different languages share vocabulary terms. Cognates (also known as *word twins*) are words that are similar to words in your language. If a word in English appears similar to a word in your language, see if the meaning makes sense in the sentence. If it does, you have found a cognate.

> **Example:** English: *indifference*   French: *indifférence*   Spanish: *indiferencia*

False Cognates

Sometimes words look alike but have different meanings in different languages. For example, a form of *gentle* appears in many Latin-based languages. In English, it means "mild; not rough," but in French, *gentil* means "nice."

Reading Exercise

The following paragraphs contain words that may be similar to words in your language. As you read, underline any cognates. Also look for words that appear similar, but may have different meanings.

> Fads follow a common pattern. They appear quickly, and they occupy the attention of people across the country. Then, just as quickly as they arrive, they fade away. Fads may involve products, fashions, or activities. Occasionally, a fad disappears, and then it resumes its popular position a few years later.

> Some fads appear useful, but they actually have no valuable purpose. Circular apple slicers, for instance, appeared to make the cutting of apples simpler, and millions of people bought them. However, customers quickly realized that it is actually faster to cut an apple using an ordinary knife than it is to use the apple slicer.

> Marketers often manipulate consumers by implying that a product has a very limited quantity. For example, in 1998, Tyko Toys warned that there were not enough Tickle-Me-Elmos to face the great demand. You might think that sensible consumers would not be fooled. However, most consumers are not very sensible. In a panic, customers rushed to toy stores to buy the Elmo doll, and the company's prediction came true when stores ran out of the product.

Complete the following chart. Identify at least four cognates and two false cognates in the text.

WORD FROM THE TEXT	THE WORD IN MY LANGUAGE	THE MEANING: same	different
1. _____	_____	☐	☐
2. _____	_____	☐	☐
3. _____	_____	☐	☐
4. _____	_____	☐	☐
5. _____	_____	☐	☐
6. _____	_____	☐	☐
7. _____	_____	☐	☐
8. _____	_____	☐	☐

Team Reading Activity (Optional)

Form a group of three students. Each of you should read one of the following sections:

• Product Fads

• Fashion Fads

• Activity Fads

Answer the comprehension questions about your part of the text. Later you will share your information with other students.

Reading 3.1

Fads appear in many different forms. Groups of people may decide to buy a useless product, take part in an activity that appears nonsensical, or dress in bizarre and unattractive clothing. In the next readings, you will learn about some common fads and fashions. As you read, underline three or four cognates (words that look like words in your language).

Product, Fashion, and Activity Fads

Part 1: Product Fads

1 Product fads include toys, games, household items, car decorations, or any other product that becomes immensely popular. Sometimes, large numbers of people decide to buy a useless item simply because everyone else has it.

2 In 1909, the kewpie doll fad occurred. Children's author Rose O'Neill illustrated her stories with wide-eyed characters she called "Kewpies." Named after Cupid, kewpies had big cheeks, round tummies, and one small tuft of hair on their heads. During a four-year period, millions of kewpie dolls were sold.

>>> Kewpie doll

3 Some product fads had useful purposes. In 1958, a toy company marketed a long tube of plastic shaped like a circle. People placed hula hoops on their waists and gyrated their hips like a hula dancer to make the hoop rotate. Thus, the hula hoop actually served a purpose and helped people stay in shape. In a one-year period, the Whammo toy company sold twenty-five million hoops.

>>> Hula hoop

4 In 1975, one of the silliest fads occurred. An entrepreneur in San Francisco placed an ordinary rock in a cardboard box and labelled the creation a "Pet Rock." Soon, a toy company marketed the item. Each rock came with an owner's manual and a birth certificate, and it sold for about four dollars. There was nothing particularly special about the rocks, yet, in a one-year period, over five million people bought them!

5 In the mid 1970s, the CB radio craze occurred. CBs, or citizen's band radios, could receive and transmit messages. Drivers installed CBs in their cars and used them to alert each other to police traps. Truckers used the radios to communicate with others and feel less lonely.

6 In 1996, a new toy craze began in Japan, and quickly crossed the globe. People bought a small "virtual pet" called a Tamagotchi. The toy was the size of an egg, and on a small screen there was a tiny bird or some other animal. The owner had to press buttons in order to feed and clean up after the pet. If the owner forgot to push the buttons, the animated pet would die.

>>> CB radio

Comprehension

Using your own words, define the following product fads. Mention when each fad was popular.

1• Kewpie doll _____

_____

2 • Hula hoop _____

_____

3 • Pet rock _____

_____

4 • CB radio _____

_____

5 • Tamagotchi _____

_____

>>> Bouffant hairdo

Part 2: Fashion Fads

1 Fashions evolve over time. Fads, on the other hand, occur when large numbers of people suddenly decide to have the same hairstyle, clothing, or body art for a short period of time.

2 Throughout history, there are examples of fashion fads relating to hairstyles. For example, when French King Louis XIV started to go prematurely bald, he wore large curly wigs. Soon, fashionable men across France covered their heads in large heavy wigs. More recently, in the 1960s, the bouffant hairdo became a fashion fad. Women used heavy sprays in order to puff their hair up into a ball on their heads. Some even added fake hairpieces to give their hair added height.

3 Some fashion fads signalled a change in status. In the 1890s, when women began getting certain rights, bloomers became a fashion fad. Bloomers were baggy pants that women wore alone or under long skirts. Women could hike their skirts up and engage in activities such as bicycle riding.

4 In the 1940s, zoot suits became popular among young men. The zoot suits had very long suit jackets that were broad at the shoulders and narrow at the waist. The pants were baggy, but very narrow at the ankles. Zoot suits were associated with jazz music and crime.

5 In the 1980s, leg warmers were a popular fashion fad. Millions of women wore long socks (without feet) over their pants or stockings. Then, as quickly as the leg warmer fad began, it ended.

6 Many fashion fads involve shoes. In the 1950s, tough young men attached moon-shaped pieces of steel onto the heels of their shiny black shoes. When they walked into school, their "tap" shoes made a tapping sound in the hallways. In the mid 1970s, platform shoes became popular. Young men and women walked in shoes with soles of about six inches in height. Some rock stars of the era tried to come up with the tallest shoes possible. Singer Elton John and the rock band Kiss tottered around in twenty-inch-high shoes.

>>> Zoot suit

>>> Platform shoes

Comprehension

Using your own words, define the following fashion fads. Mention when each fad was popular.

1 • Curly wig _____

_____

2 • Bouffant hair _____

_____

3 • Bloomers _____

_____

4 • Zoot suit _____

_____

5 • Platform shoes _____

_____

Part 3: Activity Fads

1 An activity fad occurs when people suddenly take up a new leisure activity that would otherwise be unappealing. In the 1920s, for instance, the dance marathon fad occurred. In school gymnasiums and nightclubs, couples entered contests to see which couple could spend the longest period of time dancing. Allowing for short food breaks, the longest dance marathon lasted three weeks.

2 The flagpole-sitting fad occurred in 1924. Alvin Kelly sat on a flagpole for over thirteen hours. Within weeks, people across North America tried to break the flagpole-sitting record. Huge crowds gathered to watch the participants. Near the end of the fad, Alvin Kelly decided that he wanted to regain his record, so he sat on a flagpole for forty-nine days in front of thousands of people.

3 In 1938, the goldfish-swallowing fad began. A Harvard University student named Lothrop Withington Jr. swallowed a goldfish on a dare, and the Boston media publicized the event. Within weeks, students in other cities started swallowing the tiny fish. One record-holder allegedly sucked down 300 fish in one sitting. The fad, like many activity fads, ended as quickly as it began.

4 The 1950s saw the phone-booth stuffing fad, which began in South Africa when twenty-five students squeezed themselves into a small phone booth. Soon, college students in North America and England copied the fad. They followed precise rules: all body parts must be inside the booth, and somebody inside the booth must place a phone call.

5 In 1974, the streaking fad became popular. On college campuses, students removed all of their clothing and ran through public places such as football fields and malls. During the 1974 Academy Awards, a nude streaker dashed behind presenter David Niven. Within two years, college kids lost the desire to strip and run naked in public places.

>>> Flagpole sitting

>>> Goldfish swallowing

>>> Phone-booth stuffing

6 Some activity fads are extremely dangerous. Bungee jumping, which had a surge of popularity in the 1990s, has caused several deaths. Some free divers, who descend to extreme depths under water while holding their breaths, have also lost their lives.

Sources: Badfads.com; David A. Locher. *Collective Behavior*. Prentice Hall.

Comprehension

Using your own words, define the following activity fads. Mention when each fad was popular.

1 • Dance marathon _____

_____

2 • Flagpole sitting _____

_____

3 • Goldfish swallowing _____

_____

4 • Phone-booth stuffing _____

_____

5 • Streaking _____

_____

Share Information

To work on your writing skills, visit the companion website.

1 • Sit with students who have read the other sections, and share information. Describe the most interesting fads to your classmates.

2 • On a separate piece of paper, list at least two cognates from each reading. Decide if the meanings are the same in your language.

Example: English: _activity_   French: _activité_   Meaning: _the same_

 Listening

---

Identify Numbers

You will hear a speaker read out some numbers. Before you listen, review how a large number is broken down.

Look at the number: **2,357,419,680**

The number breaks down as follows:

2			two billion
	357		three hundred and fifty-seven million
		419	four hundred and nineteen thousand
		680	six hundred and eighty

The speaker will say a sentence that includes a number. Write the numeral, not the word, in the space provided.

Example: _$40,000_

1. _____   6. _____
2. _____   7. _____
3. _____   8. _____
4. _____   9. _____
5. _____   10. _____

Form Present Tense Questions

You will hear some statements. Try to form a yes/no question based on those statements. After you make your own question, you will hear the correct question form. You can then check to see if you have asked the question correctly. Remember to form the question before you hear the correct form.

Example: Statement: *The moon is round.* You ask, *"Is it round?"*

After you say the question, write the correct auxiliary in the blank.

Example: _Is_ the moon round?

1. _____ Eric 19 years old?
2. _____ he have $855 in his bank account?
3. _____ the shoes cost $225?
4. _____ her hair blond?
5. _____ he spend too much on clothing?
6. _____ those prices reasonable?
7. _____ Anna spend $740 a month on rent?
8. _____ prices increase every year?
9. _____ the house expensive?
10. _____ some products useless?

Listening Extreme Sports

The sporting world has witnessed a trend toward extreme sports. Where athletes once competed to show skill and endurance, another factor has entered the sporting arena. Extreme sports athletes must conquer their fears. You will hear about the origins of some extremely dangerous sports.

Pre-Listening Vocabulary

Before you listen, read the following definitions.

- *stunt:* dangerous act
- *diving:* jumping into water head first
- *assault:* attack
- *stairs:* a set of steps to go up or down a level
- *roof:* the top covering of a building

To view a video about extreme sports, visit the companion website.

Listening Comprehension

1• Who started the extreme sports trend? _____

2• What was the name of the club that started at Oxford University?

    a) The Extreme Guys

    b) The Oxford Club

    c) The Dangerous Sports Club

3• What is BASE jumping? _____

4• In 2005, a Calgary man had an accident when he went BASE jumping and fell into the window of a building. What floor did he fall into?

    a) 10th   **b)** 15th   **c)** 24th

5• What is urban assault biking?

    a) Cyclists perform dangerous stunts in cities using stairways, etc.

    b) Cyclists ride down mountains.

    c) Cyclists ride really fast and compete to see who is the fastest.

Indicate if the following sentences are true (T) or false (F).

6• The man who tried BASE jumping and fell through a window did not survive. .... T   F

7• Urban assault cyclists sometimes jump from one roof to another. .... T   F

8• Base jumping is legal. .... T   F

9• Free divers wear oxygen masks. .... T   F

10• What is the meaning of *to black out*?

    a) to free dive   **b)** to lose consciousness   **c)** to ride a bike

11• Where do people play extreme golf?

    a) on mountainsides   **b)** in city streets   **c)** on golf greens

12• Why do people do extreme sports?

_____

_____

To develop your listening skills, visit the companion website.

Speaking •• Interview about Trends

Work with a partner.

• Add an auxiliary to each question. Insert *is, am, are, do, does, did, was,* or *were.*

• Write your partner's answers in the blanks.

    Example: What sports ___*do*___ you engage in?

             Answer: ___*baseball, running*___

Partner's name: _____

Part 1: Discussing the Past

1 • When you were younger, what _____ you look like?
Describe your hair and clothing.

Answer: _____

_____

2 • When you were a child, what product fads _____ popular? Think about
common games and toys.

Answer: _____

_____

3 • What activity fads or sports _____ you do when you were a child?

Answer: _____

_____

Part 2: Discussing the Present

4 • What _____ men and women wear today? Think about popular hair
and clothing styles.

Men's fashion fads: _____

_____

Women's fashion fads: _____

_____

5 • What product fads _____ popular today? Think about games, toys,
communication devices, and household items.

Answer: _____

_____

6 • What activity fads or extreme sports _____ people participate in these
days? An example might be extreme mountain biking.

Answer: _____

_____

Part 3: Conclusions

7 • Why _____ people follow trends? Think of two reasons.

Answer: _____

_____

Watching •• Second Life

Around the world, people are creating fascinating new lives for themselves online in a place called Second Life. Millions of dollars change hands, and businesses are noticing the commercial value of the virtual world. CBC reporter Adrienne Arsenault visits Second Life.

Pre-Watching Vocabulary

Before watching the video, ensure that you understand these terms.
- *wallflower:* somebody who does not get asked to dance at a dance club
- *disabled:* having a physical handicap
- *wheelchair:* special chair with wheels created for people who are unable to walk

Watching Comprehension

1• What is Adam Pasnik's job? _____

_____

2• What are Linden dollars? _____

_____

3• About how many Linden dollars make one Canadian dollar?

a) 50 **b)** 200 **c)** 300

4• What is Alison Child's job? _____

_____

5• What is an avatar? _____

6• What is the name of Adrienne Arsenault's character in Second Life?

a) Truly Magnolia **b)** Rivers Run Red **c)** Adrienne

Are the next sentences true or false? If the sentence is false, write a true sentence under it.

7• The most popular products in Second Life are shoes. ....T F

_____

8• Second Life is a crime-free world. ....T F

_____

9• Avatars can die on Second Life. ....T F

_____

10• Simon Stevens, who suffers from cerebral palsy, created a Second Life nightclub. What is the name of his nightclub?

a) Avatar **b)** Wheelies **c)** Night Time

11 • What are some negative aspects of Second Life? _____

_____

_____

12 • What are some positive aspects of Second Life? _____

_____

_____

Discussion

Over two million people have characters in Second Life. Why are virtual worlds so popular?

Reading

Reading 3.2

In the 1990s, Internet-based fads began. Many students set up their own websites, and blogging became common. When J. Kelly Nestruck was a teenager, he created a web page that he lived to regret. Read about his experiences with his "bad Google."

My Bad Google
by J. Kelly Nestruck

1 It was near the end of university that my Internet past began to catch up with me. I was out on a date with a young woman I felt particularly unworthy of when she admitted, with **nary a hint of shame**, that she had googled me the night before. I tried to take her revelation in stride, to pretend like I didn't know what she had found. But I knew. My bad Google was out of the bag.

nary a hint of shame
no embarrassment

2 I created Kelly's Pointless Homepage, my first Internet site, when I was about sixteen years old on a free web-hosting site called Geocities. Five years later, it was still the first thing to come up when you searched for my name on Google. The site revealed the truth about the dork I had been— and worried I still was.

pimply
red eruptions on the face

3 Among its many embarrassing contents, Kelly's Pointless Homepage included various pictures of my **pimply** self in my high school prefect's uniform, a list of my favourite **palindromes** ("Sex at noon taxes!"), and most damning of all, my sixteen-year-old self's list of twenty-five things that annoy me. Number 11 was "Overly masculine men." Number 12 was "Overly feminine men." Then, there was the **mortifying** Number 15: "Sexy lesbians."

palindrome
a word or sentence that is the same when read backwards or forwards

mortifying
embarrassing

4 Needless to say, this was not the image I wanted to project to the world at age twenty-one, especially on a date. I had long since come to terms with the sexy lesbians of the world and, if anything, my opinion of them had come a full 180 degrees. So that night, after nervously laughing off the Internet excesses of my youthier youth, I decided that Kelly's Pointless Homepage—and by extension, my sixteen-year-old self—must die.

5 Trying to delete the web page the next day, however, I found myself **outwitted** by my younger self. I could not for the life of me remember the password to edit or take down the site. Did it have something to with *The X-Files*? Perhaps it had something to do with the Donald Duck comic books I collected at the time? Geocities customer service would send me the password, but only to the long **defunct** e-mail address I had used to sign up for the web page. Stuck, I had to learn how to live with Kelly's Pointless Homepage for the time being.

outwitted
skilfully manipulated

defunct
obsolete or invalid

6 When I entered the workforce, however, my bad Google began to haunt me in a potentially career-damaging way. During my initial internship with this newspaper, someone on the *Frank* magazine on-line forum linked to my Pointless Homepage and made fun of it. "You're just **ludicrous** ... quit journalism while you're ahead," one anonymous meanie wrote.

ludicrous
absurd and ridiculous

7 I began to wonder: How long would this web page haunt me? Was it possible that someday, my grandson might tug on my pant leg, look up with that little cherubic face of his and ask, "Grandpa, why do you hate sexy lesbians?"

8 It was time for definitive action and, luckily, I had become a little craftier than I was in university. I e-mailed Yahoo! (which had purchased Geocities at this point) and told them that they were hosting my copyrighted material without my permission. If they didn't take down Kelly's Pointless Homepage in a week, they would hear from my (imaginary) lawyer. Within a day, it was gone.

9 And that's how I finally triumphed over my teenage self and saved myself from my bad Google. Now, if only I could replace some of the pages in the family photo albums with "Sorry, the page you requested was not found."

Verb Hunt

1 • The following past tense verbs appear in Paragraph 1. Complete each verb. Then write the present-tense form of the verb. The first one is done for you.

PAST	PRESENT	PAST	PRESENT
a) w_a_ _s_	_is_	**d)** a_ _ _ _ _ed	_____
b) b_ _ _ _	_____	**e)** t_ _ _ _	_____
c) f_ _ _	_____	**f)** k_ _ _	_____

Vocabulary •• Using Context Clues

2• *Worthy* means "important" or "deserving respect." In Paragraph 1, what is the meaning of *unworthy*?

_____

3• Google is an Internet search engine. In Paragraph 1, what is the meaning of *googled*?

_____

4• In Paragraph 2, what is a *dork*?

   a) a popular guy   **b)** a nerd or unpopular guy   **c)** a hero

5• In Paragraph 7, what does *tug* mean? _____

6• Find a word in Paragraph 8 that means "smarter and more devious."

   _____

Comprehension

7• What is the article about? _____

_____

8• What embarrassing content was on Kelly's old Internet site?

_____

_____

9• What problem(s) did the old website cause for Kelly?

   a) A girl that he dated said that she looked at his website.

   b) At work, somebody found his site and ridiculed him.

   c) A lawyer contacted him and asked him to remove his site.

   d) Both a) and b)

10• What is true about Paragraph 5?

   a) Kelly remembered the password to his Internet site.

   b) Kelly's password had a relation to Donald Duck comic books.

   c) Kelly did not remove Kelly's Pointless Homepage at that time.

   d) Kelly continues to use his old email address.

11• How did Kelly finally solve his problem and remove his old website?

_____

_____

_____

12• What is the moral of the story? What message does his story have for the reader?

_____

_____

Speaking •• Present a Trend

Work with a partner. Try to predict or invent a new trend, or choose an old trend that could be popular again. Think about a product, fashion, or activity trend.

For example, you can present a hairdo, a new clothing style, an extreme sport, a game, or a great product. Then prepare a short commercial to advertise that trend. Remember that you do not have to invent a new trend. You can reintroduce a trend that is no longer popular. Your goal is to convince the audience that they should try that trend.

Option: If you have access to video equipment, film your commercial. It should be about two minutes in length. You can include interviews with people who love the trend.

When you finish your presentation, your classmates may ask you questions about the trend.

Writing Topics

Write about one of the following topics. When you finish writing, refer to the relevant checklist on the inside back cover.

1 • Write about past and present fads. In one paragraph, describe some activity, product, or fashion fads that you followed when you were a child. In a second paragraph, describe some fads that people follow today.

2 • Write about trends. Why do people follow trends? Give at least two reasons and provide examples for each reason.

3 • Explain why it is important to be careful when you create a web page or any other content for the Internet.

4 • Write about something that really annoys you. Explain why it annoys you.

5 • Write an essay about virtual worlds. In one paragraph, describe the world of Second Life. In another paragraph, explain the benefits and disadvantages of virtual worlds.

To review some of the vocabulary studied in this chapter, visit the companion website.

Warm Up •• Physical Descriptions (continued from page 34)

The Arts

.. *Art is a lie that makes us realize the truth.* ..

Pablo Picasso

What does the opening quotation mean? In this chapter you will read about some people who were artistic geniuses.

Warm Up .. Arts Trivia Game

Join a group of four to six students. Write the names of your team members.

Team members:

_____   _____   _____

_____   _____   _____

Look at the three clues. Then try to guess the name of each song, movie, singer, television show, and so on. Use a dictionary if you don't understand some words.

| | **Example:** | Dion | *Titanic* | megahit | ▶ | Song: *My Heart Will Go On* |

1• Neo   blue pill   Morpheus   ▶ Movie: _____

2• Armorica   Gaul   funny   ▶ Comics: _____

3• cavemen   gravel pit   cartoon   ▶ TV show: _____

4• French   "Complicated" Nepean,   ▶ Singer: _____
   name   Ontario

5• Latin   romantic   rhymes with   ▶ Dance: _____
                               mango

6• quidditch   Hogwarts   Malfoy   ▶ Novels: _____

7• big lips   adoptions   *Mr. and   ▶ Actress: _____
                               Mrs. Smith*

8• AIDS   tenants   musical   ▶ Play/Movie: _____

9• teen spirit   Seattle   April 5, 1994   ▶ Musician: _____

10• Ludwig   German   deaf   ▶ Composer: _____

11• moustache   melting clock   surrealist   ▶ Artist: _____

12• queen   Freddy Mercury   winners   ▶ Song: _____

13• jewelry   dwarves   Frodo   ▶ Novels: _____

14• Billie Joe   *American Idiot*   *Nimrod*   ▶ Band: _____

15• Betty   Veronica   Jughead   ▶ Comics: _____

16• totem pole   West Coast   college   ▶ Artist: _____

17• Stewie   Brian the dog   Quahog   ▶ TV show: _____

18• Jim's dad   dessert   Stifler   ▶ Movie: _____

19• toe shoes   Bolshoi   Nutcracker   ▶ Dance style: _____

20• pirate   lives in France   Scissorhands   ▶ Actor: _____

21• baseball cap   *Fahrenheit 9/11*   documentaries   ▶ Filmmaker: _____

22• blond   Columbian   "La Tortura"   ▶ Singer: _____

23• 1996 death   gang shooting   *Juice*   ▶ Rapper: _____

24• Blue Period   Spanish   cubist   ▶ Artist: _____

25• Canadian   *Mask*   pet dectective   ▶ Actor: _____

26• piano   "Above us only sky"   Lennon   ▶ Song: _____

Reading

Reading **Strategy**

Summarizing Main Ideas

A summary is a review of a text's main ideas. In a summary, you include the overall main idea, but you also include the text's most relevant supporting points. When you summarize, you restate what the author said using your own words.

How to Summarize

- **Select the most important ideas.** Read the text and identify key information. Do not worry about details.

To practise your speaking skills, visit the companion website.

- **Take notes.** Only write down single words or short phrases.
- **Put aside the original source.** Write your summary from memory and refer to your notes. Avoid looking at the original source.
- **Verify that you have not copied exact phrases or sentences** from the original text.
- **Do not give your opinion.**

Plagiarism

Do not copy exact phrases or sentences from another author. When you summarize, always restate information using your own words.

For example, read a summary of the following paragraph.

Original Work

Jim Carrey was born in Newmarket, Ontario, on January 17, 1962, and his comic spirit was evident at an early age. In a Grade 2 music class, while Carrey was misbehaving, his exasperated music teacher asked him to perform in front of the class. The teacher, who hoped to embarrass Jim, ended up laughing with the rest of the class as he danced and played an imaginary violin. Later, Carrey's Grade 7 teacher says that she was able to control his exuberant spirit by allowing him to entertain his classmates at the end of the day in exchange for his good behaviour.

Summary

Jim Carrey was not a model student, and he often disturbed his classmates. Some of his teachers tried to integrate his humour into their classes.

Reading Exercise

Read the following paragraph from a biography of Marilyn Monroe.

Born on June 1, 1926, in Los Angeles, California, Norma Jeane had a mentally unstable mother and her father was absent. She spent her first seven years living with foster parents: "They were terribly strict … It was their religion. They brought me up harshly." She spent the rest of her childhood living with her mother's friend, Grace, and she spent two years in an orphanage. Later, in interviews, she would lie about her childhood and say that she was an orphan, perhaps out of shame at her mother's illness and institutionalization.

In one or two sentences, write the main points of the paragraph. Use your own words, and do not copy any sentences or phrases!

_____

_____

_____

_____

Pair Reading Activity (Optional)

Find a partner. One of you could read "Biography of Vincent Van Gogh," and the other could read "Frida: Mexico's Passion."

Answer the questions that follow your reading. Later, you will share information with your partner.

Reading 4.1

Read the following biography. Don't stop at difficult words. Your goal is to identify main events in Vincent Van Gogh's life.

Biography of Vincent Van Gogh

•• In a picture I want to say something comforting, as music is comforting. I want to paint men and women with that something of the eternal that the halo used to symbolize. ••

Vincent Van Gogh

Vincent Van Gogh's self-portrait

1 Sometimes children display signs of genius or of exceptional talent in a specific field. Tiger Woods, for instance, was obsessed with golf, and as a three-year-old child he was capable of executing complicated golf strokes. He went on to become a wealthy and renowned expert in his field. However, some of the world's most astounding and creative personalities were considered failures in their lifetimes. Vincent Van Gogh was such a man. Van Gogh had a major influence on modern art, but he lived a short and unhappy life and never really considered himself to be a success.

2 Vincent Van Gogh was born in Zundert, the Netherlands, in 1853. At the age of sixteen, he went to work in his uncle's art gallery in London. He rented a room in a rooming house, and he fell in love with his landlord's daughter. She already had a fiancé, and she made it clear that she had no interest in Vincent. That was his first rejection in love, and he became increasingly solitary.

3 When Van Gogh was twenty-seven, he met his cousin Kay who was a widow with a small child. He declared his love for Kay, but she, too, rejected him. When Vincent finally met a woman who returned his love, the romance failed. Her family didn't like the poverty-stricken painter.

4 Van Gogh tried a variety of professions. In addition to his job as a salesman in an art gallery, he also worked as a bookseller, a French tutor, and a missionary. In his twenties, he ministered to the poor in a coal-mining district in southwestern Belgium. He became extremely concerned about the people in his district, and he stopped eating so that he could give more money to the poor. Eventually he gave away all of his clothing and possessions. He was fired from the ministering job because his superiors felt that he displayed "excessive enthusiasm."

5 By age twenty-seven, Van Gogh felt like a failure. He was unable to keep a job, he was unlucky in love, and his faith in his religion was weakened.

6 Penniless and in despair, he isolated himself and began to draw. With the financial support of his brother, Theo, Vincent made dark and sober paintings of peasant families. Then, as his skills developed, his colours became brighter and more vibrant. He painted flowers, landscapes, and self-portraits. His vigorous brush strokes and thick application of paint made his work unique.

Van Gogh's bedroom in Arles (1889)

7 Vincent Van Gogh eventually settled in southern France, in Arles, where he bought a yellow house. He wanted to start an artist's colony, and he invited the painter Paul Gauguin to share the house with him. Gauguin came, but he and Van Gogh had a violent relationship. After two months, Van Gogh suffered an attack of delirium and attacked Gauguin with a razor. Filled with remorse, Vincent then cut off the bottom portion of his own left ear.

8 In 1889, feeling increasingly worried about his sanity, Vincent requested to stay in an asylum in Saint-Rémy. He spent twelve months under medical supervision, and during this period his colours became calmer. In December 1889, he wrote a letter to his friend Emile Bernard: "I have just done five size 30 canvasses of olive trees. And the reason I am staying on here is that my health is improving a great deal."

9 Vincent's brother, Theo, continued to support Vincent both economically and morally. However, Vincent became increasingly lonely and depressed about his economic reliance on his married brother.

10 In 1890, just six months after stating that his health was "improving a great deal," Van Gogh committed suicide by shooting himself.

11 At his death, the name of Vincent Van Gogh was unknown. During his lifetime he produced about 750 paintings and 1,600 drawings, yet he sold only one painting for a very low price.

12 Today, Van Gogh's paintings are worth millions of dollars. For example, in 1990, *The Portrait of Dr. Gachet* sold for $82.5 million (US). Unfortunately, Vincent Van Gogh never realized that he would become a valued and influential artist.

Sources: Encyclopaedia Britannica, 15th Edition, Volume 5. (1988)
All about artists at www.allaboutartists.com/bios/vangogh.html
Vincent Van Gogh gallery biography at www.vangoghgallery.com/misc/bio.htm
Van Gogh Gallery at http://192.41.62.196//misc/bio.htm

Verb Hunt

1 • Look at the last sentence in Paragraph 3: *Her family didn't like the poverty-stricken painter.*

   a) What is the auxiliary? _____

   b) What is the main verb? _____

   c) Why doesn't the main verb end in *ed*? _____

2 • Look at Paragraphs 2 and 3. Underline all past tense verbs (except *was* or *were*). Then, in the box below, write down five regular past tense verbs and six irregular past tense verbs. Also write the base form of each verb.

REGULAR VERBS		IRREGULAR VERBS	
BASE FORM	**PAST FORM**	**BASE FORM**	**PAST FORM**
a) *rent*	*rented*	a) *go*	*went*
b)		b)	
c)		c)	
d)		d)	
e)		e)	
		f)	

Comprehension

3 • When was Vincent Van Gogh born? _____

4 • Write three adjectives that describe Van Gogh. _____

_____

5 • How many paintings did he produce during his lifetime? _____

6 • Van Gogh was fired from his minister's job for "excessive enthusiasm." In your own words, explain why he was fired.

_____

_____

7 • Who was Theo? _____

8 • Why did Vincent Van Gogh feel like a failure? _____

_____

Identify Important Points

9 • List the *main* events in Vincent Van Gogh's life. Do not worry about details. Try to do this from memory.

- *Van Gogh was born in the Netherlands in 1853.*

- *Women rejected him.*

- _____

- _____

- _____

- _____

- _____

- _____

- _____

Reading 4.2

Read the following biography. Don't stop at difficult words. Your goal is to identify main events in Frida Kahlo's life.

Frida: Mexico's Passion

>>> Frida Kahlo and Diego Rivera

1 One of the world's greatest female painters was born on July 6, 1907, to an upper-class Mexican family. Frida Kahlo, the daughter of a German Jew and a part-Indian, part-Spanish mother, became famous for her intensely personal, often painful self-portraits.

2 Early on, Frida Kahlo proved to be a flamboyant character. Conscious of her effect on others, she enjoyed dressing outrageously. She would wear men's suits or colourful peasant dresses and put flowers in her hair.

3 Kahlo met the great Mexican painter Diego Rivera when he was commissioned to paint a mural for her high school. She had a schoolgirl crush on the older painter, and she told her school friends that she would marry Rivera one day. After he finished the mural, Kahlo did not see the painter for several years.

4 When she was eighteen, an accident occurred that dramatically altered her life. A streetcar hit the bus she was riding in. The bus shattered to pieces, and a handrail went through Kahlo's body. She eventually regained her ability to walk, but the accident caused her to suffer serious health problems for the rest of her life. She was often in pain and had to be hospitalized for long periods of time. Additionally, she told others that she felt extremely lonely during that period. To cope with her intense physical suffering, she turned to alcohol and medications.

5 During her two-year convalescence, Frida's mother gave her a special easel, and Frida learned to paint while lying down. At age twenty, when she was able to walk again, she presented some of her artwork to Diego Rivera. The great artist encouraged her and told her that her self-portraits were especially original.

6 Even though Diego Rivera was much older than Frida, they fell in love and married on August 21, 1929. Many of Frida's friends were surprised that she would marry the overweight, middle-aged artist. However, the couple shared a passion for art, communism, and indigenous cultures.

7 The Kahlo-Rivera marriage was stormy. Diego was a womanizer and, after several years of marriage, he pursued Frida's younger sister, Cristina. Perhaps to retaliate for Diego's romance with her sister, Frida embarked on a series of affairs with both men and women. She had a scandalous affair with the Communist leader Leon Trotsky when he was a guest at her home. At one point, Frida and Diego divorced for a year and then remarried. Frida once called the streetcar and Diego the two main accidents of her life.

8 In her art, Frida Kahlo painted self-portraits that often depicted her anger and despair. Her portraits included surreal elements. For example, in a powerful image, she depicted two versions of herself with her heart and veins exposed. In another image, she is shown giving birth to herself.

9 Parisian surrealists discovered Kahlo's art, and in 1938 they invited her to exhibit her paintings in France. Her appearance, with her long, colourful dresses and exotic jewelry, attracted a lot of attention. André Breton, Pablo Picasso, and Marcel Duchamp paid tribute to her beauty and talent, and the Louvre purchased one of her paintings.

10 Although Frida Kahlo did not enjoy the same level of respect and fame as Diego Rivera, she attained a certain level of critical success during her lifetime. In 1953, the Mexican National Institute of Fine Arts held a retrospective of Frida Kahlo's art. She arrived at the exhibition by ambulance and was carried to a canopied bed in the centre of the crowded room. She entertained the crowd with her stories and jokes, and the exhibition was an astounding success.

11 During the last year in her life, Kahlo's leg had to be amputated due to gangrene, and she fell into a heavy depression. Just seven days after her forty-seventh birthday, Frida Kahlo died. Although her death certificate attributed the death to natural causes, many believe that she may have committed suicide or accidentally over-dosed on drugs. Because no autopsy was performed, the true cause of her death is uncertain.

Sources: Zamora, Martha. *Frida Kahlo, The Brush of Anguish.* San Francisco: Chronicle Books, 1990.
Frida Kahlo and Contemporary Thoughts at www.fridakahlo.it/
Las Mujeres: Frida Kahlo at www.lasmujeres.com/fridakahlo/
Frida Kahlo tribute site at http://members.tripod.com/ritzobrian/kahlo.html

Verb Hunt

1 • In Paragraph 5 there are two past forms of the verb *be*. Write down the subject and each form of the verb *be*.

Subject	Form of *be*	Subject	Form of *be*

2 • Look at Paragraph 4. Underline all verbs that are in the simple past tense (except *was* and *were*). Then, in the box below, write down six regular and five irregular past tense verbs. Also write the base form of each verb.

REGULAR VERBS		IRREGULAR VERBS	
BASE FORM	PAST FORM	BASE FORM	PAST FORM
a) *occur*	*occurred*	a) *hit*	*hit*
b)		b)	
c)		c)	
d)		d)	
e)		e)	
f)			

Vocabulary and Comprehension

3 • Read the following definitions of the word *affair*. What is the meaning of *affair* in Paragraph 7?

a) a public event

b) personal business matters

c) a romance outside marriage

4 • Write three adjectives that describe Frida Kahlo. _____
_____

5 • How did the streetcar accident change Frida's life? _____
_____

6 • What did Frida Kahlo and Diego Rivera have in common? _____
_____

7 • How was Frida's marriage "stormy"? _____
_____

8 • What types of paintings did Frida create? _____
_____

9 • Was Kahlo respected for her artwork during her lifetime? Explain your answer.
_____
_____

Identify Important Points

10 • List the *main* events in Frida Kahlo's life. Do not worry about details. Try to do this from memory.

- *Frida was born to a rich Mexican family.* _____
- *She was original and wore interesting clothing.* _____
- _____
- _____
- _____
- _____
- _____
- _____
- _____

Fell, Felt, and *Failed*

Sometimes you may confuse the following verbs. Review the present and past forms of each verb.

Present	Past	Example
fall	*fell*	You **fall** down. Yesterday, the baby **fell** out of its chair.
feel	*felt*	She **feels** happy. Yesterday, she **felt** angry.
fail	*failed*	Someone **fails** a test. Ben **failed** the test yesterday.

A list of irregular past tense verbs appears in the appendix of *Open Book English Grammar*.

To perfect your reading skills, visit the companion website.

Pair Reading •• Share Your Information

To answer the questions, work with a student who has read the other reading.

1• Write down the past forms of the following verbs.

tell _____   feel _____   meet _____

fail _____   fall _____   have _____

2• Compare Vincent Van Gogh with Frida Kahlo. Discuss the following points with your partner. Write down information in the chart.

	VINCENT VAN GOGH	FRIDA KAHLO
Love		
Health		
Relationship with brother/sister		
Types of paintings		
Artistic success during his or her lifetime		

Watching ·· A Brief History of Reggae

>>> Bob Marley

When you watch the DVD, you will learn a brief history of reggae.

Pre-Watching Vocabulary

Before watching, read the following vocabulary definitions.
- *slum*: poor and crowded area of a city
- *faith*: a strong belief in something

Watching for Vocabulary

Watch the introduction to "A Brief History of Reggae."
Fill in the blanks with one of the following words:

popular	global	greatest	homeland	music	village

1 • Bob Marley was a _____ superstar. *Time* magazine named his 1977 album *Exodus* the _____ album of the twentieth century. But Marley viewed the global entertainment industry as an agent of Babylon, the imperialism and oppression his _____ sought to overcome.

2 • Marley's music was popular, first in his Jamaican _____, and then internationally. Like other forms of _____ culture, it carries a message that speaks to a broad spectrum of people, one of the ways that popular culture influences today's _____.

Watching Comprehension

3 • Who was Marcus Garvey?
   a) a reggae singer   **b**) a music producer   **c**) a Jamaican preacher

4 • What is true about the Rastafarian faith?
   a) The name came from Ras Tafari who later became Emperor Haile Selassie.
   b) It began in the 1930s.
   c) It began in Jamaica.
   d) Rastafarians believed that their leader was a descendant of King David.
   e) All of the answers.

5 • When did Jamaica become independent from Britain?
   a) 1930   **b**) 1962   **c**) 1977

6 • What did the word *reggae* originally mean in Jamaican English?
   a) dance hard   **b**) coming from the people   **c**) the harder they come

7 • Which film helped reggae become popular?
   a) *Never Grow Old*   **b**) *Do the Reggae*   **c**) *The Harder They Come*

8 • Where did Bob Marley and the Wailers come from?

    a) the slums of Kingston   **b)** Ethiopia   **c)** the United States

9 • How did reggae differ from other popular music? _____

_____

10 • Which nation's flag did Bob Marley display at his concerts?

    a) Ethiopia   **b)** Jamaica   **c)** Kenya

Speaking •• Describe Objects

Review the following vocabulary words. Ask your teacher or use a dictionary to find the meanings of unfamiliar words.

circular	hard	oval	rough	smooth	stiff	wide
fabric	metal	plastic	round	soft	thick	wood
flat	narrow	rectangular	rubber	square	thin	

Now work with a team of students. You will reach into a bag and touch an object that other classmates cannot see. Do not show the object to your classmates.

Describe the object for your classmates. Do not say what the object is used for. Only describe what the object looks or feels like. Use your dictionary if you do not know how to say a word. Then your classmates will guess what the object is.

Reading

Reading 4.3

In this chapter you have learned about famous artists. Now read about a famous Canadian performer. As you read, underline important words or phrases. On a separate piece of paper, keep notes. Later, you will summarize this reading, and you should not look at the original source!

Canada's Funny Man

1 If you ask people what they think of Canadians, a few adjectives repeatedly pop up. Canadians are "nice." We are "reserved." We are "polite." But most won't call Canadians funny. Yet no country produces as many internationally famous comedians as this sparsely populated northern country.

2 Lorne Michaels, Andrea Martin, Eugene Levy, Phil Hartman, Michael J. Fox, Leslie Nielsen, John Candy, Rick Moranis, and Martin Short are just some Canadian comics who have become internationally known. Even Mike Myers, known for his Austin Powers

films, was born in Scarborough, Ontario. But did you know that the world's most instantly recognizable comedian, Jim Carrey, is also Canadian?

Jim Carrey

3 Jim Carrey was born in Newmarket, Ontario, on January 17, 1962, and his comic spirit was evident at an early age. In a Grade 2 music class, while Carrey was misbehaving, his exasperated music teacher asked him to perform in front of the class. The teacher, who hoped to embarrass Jim, ended up laughing with the rest of the class as he danced and played an imaginary violin. Later, Carrey's Grade 7 teacher says that she was able to control his exuberant spirit by allowing him to entertain his classmates at the end of the day in exchange for his good behaviour.

4 Carrey may have laughed at school, but his home life was tough. When Jim was a teenager, his dad lost his job and was unable to pay the mortgage on the family home. The whole family moved to Scarborough, Ontario, to work as janitors in a factory. For a year, Jim tried to juggle work and school, but in Grade 9 he dropped out and went to work full time. By the age of fifteen, he was working at Toronto comedy clubs. He admits that he was an angry loner during those difficult years, but comedy helped him cope.

5 Jim Carrey moved to the United States in his early twenties. During a stay in Los Angeles, he hopefully wrote a $20 million cheque to himself. At the time, he was simply dreaming of fame and fortune. Of course, his dream became reality a few years later!

6 However, Carrey's path to fame wasn't instant. He was booed off more than one stage. At a 1990 audition for *Saturday Night Live* (the television comedy show that hired Canadian comics like Eugene Levy, Mike Myers, and John Candy) Jim Carrey was rejected. And his first television show, *The Duck Factory*, only lasted for a few months.

7 Jim Carrey's big break came when he found work as "the white guy" on *In Living Colour*. He created a series of characters for the show, including Fire Marshall Bill and Vero De Milo. Then, in 1994, he received $175,000 for his role in *Ace Ventura, Pet Detective*. The film had a low budget and low expectations, but it went on to make millions of dollars. Subsequent films such as *The Mask* and *Dumb and Dumber* ensured Jim's superstar status.

8 Carrey can do more than just make people laugh. He did a dramatic role as the innocent Truman Burbank in *The Truman Show*. He also won critical acclaim for his role in *Eternal Sunshine of the Spotless Mind*.

9 Carrey has come a long way since his days cleaning factory floors. His wild comedy style, his rubber face, and his trademark comment, "Alrighty then," have all helped make Jim Carrey a household name. So, the next time you hear that Canadians are reserved and boring, remember that Canada produces some of the world's funniest people!

Sources: Falcone, Jeremy. *AbsoluteNow,* "Jim Carrey biography," www.absolutecelebrities.com.
"The Jim Carrey Area Biography," www.geocities.com/hollywood/9090.bio
Linder, Lee. *Jim Carrey Website,* "Jim Carrey Biography," www.jimcarreywebsite.com

Write a Summary

In a paragraph of 75 to 100 words, summarize Jim Carrey's life. Refer to your notes, and do not look at the original source. Remember to use your own words. Do not plagiarize!

To work on your writing skills, visit the companion website.

Write Questions

Imagine that you could meet Jim Carrey. Write down ten questions that you would like to ask him. Use three verb tenses in your questions.

Tip Grammar

Question Form
Ensure that your questions have the proper word order.

| Question word | + | Auxiliary | + | Subject | + | Verb | + | Rest of sentence. |
| Why | | did | | you | | write | | a cheque to yourself? |

Speaking ·· Biography Project

Give a short presentation (two to three minutes) about an older friend or family member. Interview the person in order to get the following biographical information.

1. Date of birth and place of birth
2. Family situation (number of brothers and sisters)
3. Childhood: good or bad memories
4. The best moment in her/his life
5. Most valuable lesson she/he learned
6. First job, and job today
7. Favourite possession
8. Favourite music or band during adolescence
9. Dreams and goals

You do not have to speak about all of these topics! Choose the information that you find most interesting, and then speak for two minutes. If you present this to a group, other group members could ask you questions to get more information about the person.

Tip

Presentation
- You can use notes or cue cards with main words. Do not read.
- Practise your presentation.
- Time yourself. You must speak for a minimum of two minutes.
- If possible, bring in something visual. For example, if your biography subject liked a certain band, bring in a photo of that band.

Listening

Pronunciation

Part 1: Pronounce Past Tense Verbs

> **Tip**
>
> #### Pronunciation of Regular Verbs
>
> | When the verb ends in *s, k, f, x, ch,* or *sh,* the final *-ed* is pronounced *t.* | When the verb ends in *t* or *d,* the final *-ed* is pronounced as a separate syllable. | For all other regular verbs, the final *-ed* is pronounced *d.* |
> |---|---|---|
> | asked [askt] | waited [wait id] | filled [fild] |
>
> #### Pronunciation of Irregular Verbs
>
> When the verb ends in *ought* or *aught,* pronounce the final letters as *ot.*
>
> bought [bot]   taught [tot]   thought [thot]

Pronounce each set of verbs after the speaker. You will pronounce each verb in its present form and its past form. The first ten verbs are regular verbs. Numbers 11 to 15 are irregular verbs. Each set of verbs will be repeated.

Example: *talk – talked*

1. ask – asked	6. move – moved	11. have – had
2. wish – wished	7. live – lived	12. leave – left
3. hope – hoped	8. want – wanted	13. think – thought
4. walk – walked	9. add – added	14. buy – bought
5. try – tried	10. count – counted	15. teach – taught

Part 2: Pronounce Past Tense Sentences

Pronounce each sentence after the speaker. Each sentence will be repeated.

Example: I visited my mother.

1. I hoped to see him, so I asked him to visit us.
2. We talked about the problem.
3. He listened to music on the radio.
4. Last night, we waited for the train.
5. We missed the train, so we walked instead.
6. I thought I knew where the library was.
7. Yesterday we had a test, and I passed.
8. I learned a lot because my father taught me many things.
9. My father bought me a hot coffee.
10. We added up the bill, and then we left the store.

Listening Biography of John Lennon

Simon Pelletier is a Beatles enthusiast. In the following interview, Simon talks about John Lennon.

>>> John Lennon and Yoko Ono

Before you listen, discuss the following questions.
- Who were the Beatles?
- What were their names?
- Why are they still remembered today?

Listening Comprehension

Listen to the interview and then answer the questions that follow.

1 • When was John Lennon born? _____

2 • When he was a child, who did John live with?

   a) his aunt   **b)** his mother   **c)** his father

3 • How did John's mother die? _____

4 • What job did the person who hit John's mother have?

   a) taxi driver   **b)** ambulance driver   **c)** police officer

5 • What is the name of John Lennon's first wife?

   a) Yoko   **b)** Julia   **c)** Cynthia

6 • Were the Beatles instantly famous?

   a) yes   **b)** no

7 • How many marriages did John have?

   a) one   **b)** two   **c)** three

8 • Where did John meet Yoko? _____

9 • What word appeared on Yoko's painting? _____

10 • Why did John and Yoko have "bed-ins" in Toronto and Montreal?

   a) They wanted to promote their new songs.

   b) They wanted to protest war and bring attention to world peace.

   c) They wanted to bring attention to househusbands.

11 • How old was John Lennon when he died? _____

12 • What example does the speaker give to show that the Beatles are still popular?

   _____

Discussion

1 • Simon Pelletier believes that the Beatles will still be known one hundred years from now. Do you agree? Why or why not?

2 • What other musicians or bands will be famous one hundred years from now?

Speaking / Writing ·· Make an Arts Survey

Working with a team of four or five students, prepare an arts survey. Your survey can be about one of the following topics.

reading	movies	painting	drawing
architecture	dance	music	television

Working with your team members, prepare at least six questions about your topic.

• Ensure that your questions have the correct word order!

• Put a choice of answers for each question.

Examples:

Do you play a musical instrument?　　　☐ Yes　☐ No

How often do you read comic books?

a) never　　**b)** once a year　　**c)** every month　　**d)** every week

• If you ask a knowledge question, give respondents an "I don't know" choice.

Example:

Who is Martha Graham?

a) a painter　　**b)** a dancer　　**c)** an actress　　**d)** I don't know

After you have completed your questions, then one of you will remain in place, and the others will visit and survey other teams.

Writing Topics

1• Write an essay about music. In one body paragraph, you will describe somebody else's music preferences and experiences, and in the second paragraph you will describe your own.

First, ask an older friend or family member the following questions:

• What type of music did you like when you were a teenager?

• How was your favourite music similar to (or different from) today's music?

• What type of machine did you play your music on? Did you buy records, tapes, or CDs? How much did they cost?

• Did you ever try to make music (sing, play an instrument)? Why or why not?

• Do you still buy music? Why or why not?

Write about that person's music experiences. Write a second paragraph about your own music preferences and experiences.

2• Write an essay comparing Vincent Van Gogh with Frida Kahlo.

• In one paragraph, explain how Frida and Vincent are similar.

• In another paragraph, explain how Frida and Vincent are different.

3• Explain how a specific artist is or is not a good role model. The artist can be any musician, actor, dancer, painter, or writer.

To review some of the vocabulary studied in this chapter, visit the companion website.

Traditions and Celebrations

•• It is important that someone celebrate our existence. ••

Lois McMaster Bujold

In every culture, and in every era, humans have developed ceremonies and festivals. They celebrate life passages, religious events, and national holidays. In this chapter, you will learn about some particular celebrations.

Warm Up •• Holidays and Celebrations

1• Working with a group, brainstorm and list as many holidays and celebrations as you can. You can use your dictionary, if necessary.

HOLIDAYS	CELEBRATIONS
(religious, ethnic, seasonal, or national holidays and festivals) **Example:** Valentine's Day	(stage-of-life celebrations) **Example:** birthday

2• Read about some important days in countries that all have English as an official language (or as a co-official language). Guess what each holiday celebrates by writing the letter of the best description.

HOLIDAY		DESCRIPTION
1. Anzac day (April 25)	_____	a. In New Zealand, this day marks the signing of an 1840 treaty between the Aboriginal Maori people and the European settlers.
2. Robbie Burns Night (January 25)	_____	b. South Africans celebrate their 1994 elections, which marked the first time that people of all races could vote.
		c. This Australian holiday, which falls on April 25, celebrates soldiers who died in World War I at Anzac Cove.

3. Guy Fawkes' Day (November 5)	_____
4. Victoria Day (May 24)	_____
5. Freedom Day (April 27)	_____
6. Martin Luther King Day (third Monday in January)	_____
7. Waitangi Day (February 6)	_____

d. This British holiday is dedicated to a man from Yorkshire who tried to blow up the British Parliament buildings. To celebrate, the English dress up a homemade mannequin in a coat and hat and then set it on fire.

e. This holiday is celebrated in English Canada and it commemorates the birthday of the nineteenth-century British queen. Curiously, this day is not celebrated in England.

f. The Scottish celebrate their most famous poet on this evening. Traditionally, Scotch whisky is consumed and Robbie's works are read out loud.

g. In the United States, this federal holiday was officially observed for the first time in 1986. It celebrates an African American civil rights leader.

3• What are the most important celebrations or holidays in your culture?

_____

_____

Reading

Reading Strategy

To watch a video about a special holiday, visit the companion website.

Using a Dictionary

A dictionary is useful if it is used correctly. Review the following tips for proper dictionary usage.

• Look at the preface and notes in your dictionary. Your dictionary may contain a list of irregular verbs. Many dual-language dictionaries indicate the spelling of plural forms. Find out what your dictionary has to offer.

• Some words have many definitions. When you are looking up a word, do not read only the first meaning. Look for the meaning that best fits the context of your sentence.

For example, notice how a dictionary defines the word "actually."

Word-break divisions	Stress symbol (') and pronunciation	Parts of speech
Your dictionary may indicate places for dividing words with heavy black dots.	Some dictionaries provide the phonetic pronunciation of words. The stress symbol (') tells you which syllable has the highest sound.	The abbreviation means *adverb*. Look in the front or back of your dictionary for a list of parts of speech abbreviations and their meanings.

ac•tu•al•ly / ˈæktʃʊəliˌ / *adv* 1. used in order to emphasize an opinion or give new information: *Actually, a lot of Vancouver's restaurants are non-smoking.* 2. used when you are telling or asking someone what the truth about something is: *Is George actually 65?*

From the *Longman Dictionary of American English*, Pearson Education, 2000.

Reading Exercise

Examine your dictionary and answer the following questions. Choose *yes* or *no*.

1• Does your dictionary show word-break divisions? ☐ Yes ☐ No

2• Does your dictionary indicate which syllable is stressed? ☐ Yes ☐ No

3• Does your dictionary show how to spell irregular past tense verbs? (Many two-language dictionaries have an irregular verb chart. Look for it.) ☐ Yes ☐ No

Use your dictionary. Define or translate each word. Each word has more than one meaning, so list the different meanings.

4• ticket _____

_____

5• ruler _____

_____

6• trip _____

_____

Reading 5.1

Why do people play pranks on April 1? Read about the history of April Fools' Day.

The History of April Fools' Day

1 Every year on April 1, schoolchildren place tacks on their teachers' chairs, people walk around with "kick me" signs taped to their backs, and grown men and women bend down to pick up coins that have been glued to the sidewalk. While most holidays have religious or political roots, the origin of April Fools' Day is unclear.

2 Theories about April Fools' Day vary widely. Its origins may go back to ancient Rome's Hilaria Festival, which celebrated the arrival of spring. Another possible source is India's Holi (or Huli) festival. On the first full moon of March, Hindus celebrate by throwing paint and coloured powder on each other. There are songs, parades, and dances, and a sense of happiness is pervasive.

›› India's Holi festival

3 However, the most common explanation for April Fools' Day lies in France's decision to adopt a new calendar. In the early sixteenth century, French citizens celebrated the New Year for eight days, and the festivities began every March 25 and culminated with a large party on April 1. Then, in 1582 Pope Gregory XIII announced adoption of the Gregorian calendar, which celebrates New Year's Day on January 1. Some citizens didn't hear about the date change or refused to accept the new calendar, and they cheerfully continued to celebrate New Year's Day on April 1. Labelled as fools, they became victims of practical jokes, getting sent on fools' errands and invited to non-existent New Year's parties.

4 Eventually, April Fools' Day became a tradition. Citizens throughout France played pranks on friends and family members. The tradition spread to Great Britain in the eighteenth century, and then English, French, and Scottish explorers brought the festival to their colonies in America. Today, many countries celebrate a day of fun and trickery.

5 Each nation has its own peculiar way to celebrate. In France and Italy, the victims of jokes are called "April Fish" and they might have pictures of fish taped to their backs. In England, April Fools' jokes can only be played in the morning. The Scottish celebrate for two days, and the second day is called Taily Day, based on the word "tail." During Taily Day, which is devoted to jokes about the buttocks, people have animal tails or "kick me" signs taped to their rear ends.

6 Sometimes April Fools' jokes are elaborate. In 1989, British billionaire Richard Branson was responsible for an expensive gag. He arranged for a flying-saucer shaped balloon to fly over London, and he hired a very short man to assist him. When the craft landed, the small man stepped out wearing a silver alien suit, and photographers filmed the "alien" landing.

7 Members of the media also enter into the festivities. In 1957, a British television network broadcast a program about the harvesting of spaghetti from spaghetti trees. Many otherwise sensible people believed the story and called the network to ask how they could plant their own spaghetti trees. And in 1992, an American public radio station announced that disgraced former President Richard Nixon was running for office again. Once again, gullible members of the public phoned to complain about Nixon's decision, unaware that Nixon had no desire to resume his political career.

8 Corporations even get into the act. In 1998, Burger King published a full-page advertisement in *USA Today* promoting its new "Left-Handed Whopper." The hoax was a success, as thousands of customers actually tried to order the left-handed burger.

9 While many holidays involve a sprint to the shopping mall or a religious observance, April Fools' Day is a fun and stress-free celebration. The next time that April 1 rolls around, think of a harmless gag that you can play on others.

Sources: Jerry Wilson, "April Fools' Day!" (wilstar.com)
Ed Zotti, "What's the Origin of April Fools' Day?" (www.straightdope.com)
Brad Avakian, "Origin of April Fools' Day Traced to France" (The Pendulum Online)
Nat Hall, "Holi: The Fun Festival of Colours" (www.bbc.co.uk)
David Johnson, "April Fools' Day Has Serious Origins" (www.infoplease.com)

Vocabulary

1 • Try to define each word by using context clues. Then check if your definition is correct by looking in your dictionary.

a) *root* (Paragraph 1)

Your definition: _____

Dictionary definition: _____

b) *pervasive* (Paragraph 2)

Your definition: _____

Dictionary definition: _____

c) *fool* (Paragraph 3)

Your definition: _____

Dictionary definition: _____

d) *buttocks* (Paragraph 5)

Your definition: _____

Dictionary definition: _____

To work on your writing skills, visit the companion website.

e) *gag* (Paragraph 6)

Your definition: _____

Dictionary definition: _____

2 • In Paragraph 7, what is the meaning of *gullible*?

a) to act quickly   b) naive, trusting   c) distant

Comprehension •• Analyzing the Sructure

3 • Look in Paragraph 1. Underline a sentence that best sums up what the entire essay is about. (That sentence is called a thesis statement.)

4 • Each paragraph contains a topic sentence. The topic sentence describes what the paragraph is about. Underline the topic sentence in body Paragraphs 2 to 8.

Speaking •• Interview about Holidays

Work with a partner and do the following. Discuss how to form each question, and add the missing auxiliary: *do, does, is, are, did,* or *will*. Write your partner's answers in the spaces provided.

Partner's name: _____

1 • In your family or in your culture, what _____ three important holidays?

_____   _____

2 • Every year, which holiday _____ you prefer? _____

On that holiday, who do you spend time with? _____

3 • What _____ you do on your favourite holiday last year? Describe at least four things that you did.

_____

_____

_____

_____

4 • In the future, how _____ you celebrate that holiday? Explain what you will and will not do.

_____

_____

_____

5 • Why _____ all human cultures have special holidays and celebrations? Think of at least three reasons.

_____

_____

_____

_____

Writing Suggestion

Write a paragraph about your partner's significant holiday or celebration.

 Tip Grammar

Using _Will_

In the future tense, use the same form of the verb with every subject. Do not add -s to _will_ or to the verb!

       celebrate
He **will** ~~**celebrates**~~ the day with his wife.

The negative form of _will_ is _will not_ or _won't_.

      He **won't buy** too many presents for his children.

 # Reading

Reading 5.2

Mawlid Abdoul-Aziz was born and raised in Somalia. In his twenties, he left Africa and eventually settled in Montreal, Canada. In the following interview, he describes his customs.

Traditions in Somalia
An interview with Mawlid Abdoul-Aziz

>>> Mogadishu is the largest city in Somalia.

1 *What are the naming customs in Somalia?*

2 My full name is Mawlid Daoud Farah Abdoul-Aziz Ismael Farah. Actually, the name is even longer than that. In Somalia, we do not have "family name" conventions like we have here in Canada. In our tribal system, we have a series of first names of our male ancestors.

3 When we are children, we must learn the first names of our father, grandfather, great-grandfather, and so on. It helps us to know where we come from. My lineage is very long, so I memorized twenty-three first names of my father's ancestors. Remember that in my culture, people don't write as much as they speak and memorize things.

4 Somali girls have the same system. They have a given name followed by the first names of their male ancestors. When the girls get married, they have to memorize their husband's lineage because the children will have the names of the husband's ancestors.

5 *When you came to Canada, did you have to change your name?*

6 The immigration official said that I had to adopt one name as a family name. I chose my grandfather's name, which is a two-part name: Abdoul-Aziz. That is how I became Mawlid Abdoul-Aziz. It is strange to me that my grandfather's first name will now be passed along as our official family name in Canada.

7 *I would like to discuss celebrations. When you were a child, did you celebrate each birthday?*

8 No. Culturally, the day of birth is not very important. Most people don't even know their birthday. My mother could only tell me the season she was born, not the date. When I was born, births began to be registered, so people in my generation know our birthdays, but we do not have special celebrations.

9 *Are there some ceremonies for initiation?*

10 Yes, there is a celebration when boys get circumcised at about age seven. It means that the boy is becoming a man. The family throws a party and invites the relatives and neighbours. They sing local songs. The women prepare a feast with special types of food, but only males go to the party.

11 For girls, circumcision was very common all over Somalia in the past. My mother was circumcised, but the practice is now less common. Many villages made public declarations that they would no longer do female circumcision.

12 *What are some religious holidays or national holidays that you celebrate?*

13 The major celebration is Ramadan, which is during the ninth month of the Islamic calendar. It is a month that is spiritually significant. During Ramadan, we cannot eat after the sun rises, and we must fast during the entire day. We cannot even drink a glass of water. Then after sunset, we eat a large meal. We can only eat when it is dark.

14 During the month of Ramadan, we must reflect on people who do not have our advantages. By fasting, we remember those who are hungry. We must also donate money to someone who is less fortunate. It is a time of spiritual reflection.

15 *When do children begin to practise the fasting?*

16 Most children begin when they are about fifteen. It depends on each family. When I was eight, I was ready to begin. My father said I didn't have to, but I wanted to.

17 *It must be very difficult to spend a month without eating during the day.*

18 The hardest part is not having any water. You can get by without food, but it is very tough without water. It is especially difficult when Ramadan falls during the hot summer months.

19 *Can people stop the fast if they feel sick?*

20 Yes, if someone is not feeling well, they can stop the fast. Also, when women are pregnant, breastfeeding, or menstruating, they do not fast.

21 *What happens at the end of Ramadan?*

22 There is a large celebration where we buy new clothes for the children, exchange gifts, and have a large meal with the family. It is our most important celebration of the year.

Vocabulary

1 • Match the following words with their definitions. To help you choose, look at the word in context. The paragraph number is in parentheses.

TERM		DEFINITION
1. feast (10)	_____	a. to give to a charity or person in need
2. fast (13)	_____	b. not healthy
3. sunset (13)	_____	c. disappearance of the sun below the horizon
4. donate (14)	_____	d. special meal or banquet
5. sick (19)	_____	e. to abstain from eating or drinking

Comprehension •• Looking at Main Ideas

2 • In Somalia, what is the family name?

_____

_____

3 • Why did Mawlid memorize the first names of twenty-three ancestors?

_____

_____

4 • What does Mawlid do during Ramadan? Think of two things.

_____

_____

5 • For Mawlid, what is the most difficult part of Ramadan?

_____

To practise your speaking skills, visit the companion website.

Indicate if the following sentences are true or false. Circle T for "true" or F for "false."

6 • In Somalia, girls must memorize the names of their male ancestors. ......T   F

7 • Every year, Muslims celebrate Ramadan in September. ....T   F

8 • People in Somalia have special celebrations for birthdays. ....T   F

 **Listening**

Pronunciation

Practise pronouncing the following pairs of words. Pay attention to the pronunciation of *h* and *th*. You will say each pair of words twice.

> **Tip**
>
> Pronunciation
>
> When you pronounce *th*, your tongue should touch your top teeth.
>
> **Example:** bat   bath

1. tank	thank	6. ear	hear
2. it	hit	7. mat	math
3. hat	at	8. three	tree
4. air	hair	9. harm	arm
5. tear	there	10. taught	thought

Dictation

Listen to the speaker. Write each sentence in the space provided. Each sentence will be repeated.

1. _____

2. _____

3. _____

4. _____

5. _____

6. _____

7. _____

8. _____

9. _____

10. _____

Listening Hazing Rituals

In recent years, a type of initiation ritual has become common in colleges, in the military, and on sports teams. Listen to the discussion about hazing rituals.

Pre-Listening Vocabulary

Complete the next definitions by adding the appropriate word. Choose from the list.

harmless	harmful	blindfold	rookie	willing

a) A _____ is a cloth that covers a person's eyes. Then the person cannot see.

b) A _____ is a new member of a sports team.

c) Someone who is _____ gives permission or consent.

d) If something is _____, it is safe and without danger or risk.

e) If something is _____, it is not safe. It is dangerous and damaging.

Listening Comprehension

1• What is a hazing?

  a) a harmless activity to welcome new members into a group

  b) a violent or humiliating activity that is done to welcome new members into a group

2• Why was McGill in the news in 2005?

_____

3• During Laura's initiation, what did the other team members put on her?

  a) eggs   b) syrup   c) ketchup   d) all of the answers

4• Why do team members go along with the hazing? Why does nobody stop it?

_____

_____

5• Why do the team victims accept the hazing?

_____

_____

Are the next statements true or false? If the statement is false, write a true statement under it.

6• Some people have died during hazing rituals...................................T   F

_____

7• Laura was a happy and willing participant in her hazing ritual..........T   F

_____

8• The McGill football players who did hazing ritual to new players were never punished...T   F

_____

Discussion

1 • Are there any hazing rituals at your school? Are they harmless or harmful?

2 • Why do people go along with hazing rituals?

 **Reading**

Reading 5.3

In the next essay, a young black man of Lakota Sioux descent learns about giving and sharing when he undergoes an initiation ceremony. Some words are in bold. Later, you will define those words.

Pre-Reading Vocabulary

Before you read the essay, learn the meaning of the next words.

• *stickball*: a game that is similar to baseball. It is played with a piece of wood and a ball.

• *quest*: a search or expedition to find something

Naming Good Path Elk
by Kenneth M. Kline

1 I stand at the top of Morningside Park in New York City. I come to this spot whenever I'm melancholy. Here, with the warm afternoon sun massaging my skin, I consider my life. Trying to survive as a freelance journalist has only meant that I am out of work. Six months ago, I lost my uptown apartment, and creditors are showing no mercy. My name is so **tarnished**, I begin to think that my only escape is to change it. As far as I'm concerned, my good name is dead.

2 Just then a strong wind blows up from the park, quenching the hot, humid afternoon. It takes me back to a summer I spent at Camp Flying Cloud in the remote mountains around Plymouth, Vermont. I was eleven and one of fifty boys living in teepees and dressing in loincloths at the Native American camp.

3 I was **eager** to learn about the Native American blood that flowed in my African-American veins, courtesy of both my grandmothers. I had been at the camp for two weeks when Medicine Rainbow, the camp director, announced that we would begin our first naming ceremony of the summer at that night's powwow.

4 In the tradition of the Lakota Sioux, those of us selected for the naming quest would trek into the wilderness and spend three days in strict silence at a place called Blue Ledges on the edge of a mountain. There we would meditate on the names we had been given and how they would shape our lives.

5 Everyone was excited about the ceremony—except me. I had something on my mind. Earlier that week, while playing stickball, I accidentally crashed into the goalie when I was trying to score. "Look out, you moron!" he yelled, and he made **derogatory** comments about my dark skin. Before I could stop myself, I kicked him the way I had learned in karate school. He crumpled like a house of cards, and walked away crying. Then he became a target for **teasing** by other campers.

6   On the night of the powwow, I worried that the **scuffle** had tarnished my reputation—that any name I received would reflect the fight. The evening began with the lighting of a large bonfire. As the tall flames bowed and flickered in the summer breeze, a camper named Running Bull Thunders marched in, holding a long Indian pipe. He was followed by four other campers in ceremonial **garments**. Bells around their ankles rang with each step as Running Bull Thunders offered a ritual in gratitude to Mother Earth and the Four Winds. Then he seated himself before the drum at the fire's edge and began to **beat** softly: Boom-boom! Boom-boom! It was our signal to begin the powwow, our late-night dance around the campfire, singing traditional songs. Our voices and footsteps echoed in the night.

7   When the drumming stopped, we grew silent in anticipation. Suddenly a shadow broke away from the group. Known as the Stalker, he walked lightly to the fire and unrolled a red quilt with Native-American designs. Then, a shadow among shadows, he moved among us, an eagle **feather** between his fingers. He chose ten campers to be given names that night, and I was one of them.

8   The Stalker's strong hands clasped my arms as he **whispered** instructions in my ear. I was to take the eagle feather and sit cross-legged on the quilt. I held my breath as he came up behind me and daubed red paint on my temples. "Here is a boy who follows a good path like an elk crossing the woods. He is quiet and strong, always giving and helping others, and is eager to learn. For this, he shall be known as Good Path Elk." Turning solemnly to me, he added, "You must never say your name unless you become lost. Speaking your Indian name will bring a power to help you find your way."

9   Had I heard right? Had he seen me earlier in the week fighting on the stickball field? It was time for the giveaway ceremony, in which a camper volunteers to give something in friendship. Burning Eagle, an older boy I admired for his skill with Indian crafts, got to his feet. He held a woollen vest decorated with leather and seashells. Stitched on the back was an elk. "To Good Path Elk," he said, walking up to me. "This is for your naming." I was overwhelmed. I couldn't say thank you, because of the rule of silence, but I embraced him warmly.

10 The next morning, we went on a quest to Blue Ledges. I could see the mountains stretching into the distance, and I felt on top of the world. I sat on a rock and worked on a pair of leggings. As I **stitched**, a gentle breeze from the mountainside seemed to whisper my Indian name: Good Path Elk. I looked up to watch an eagle high above the valley, and a strong sense of confidence filled me.

11 At the next naming ceremony, ten more campers were chosen, among them the goalie I had kicked. His new name was Forest Talker, because he liked to talk to the plants and the trees. As I thought about the quest he and the others would begin the next morning, I had an idea. I ran back to my teepee for the leggings I had made on my quest.

12 "I'd like to give my leggings to Forest Talker," I said as the giveaway ceremony began. "This is for your naming. With these I apologize for kicking you." A few days later, Forest Talker approached me. He said, "Thanks, Good Path Elk. Those were nice leggings. Want to play a game of stickball?"

13 Now, years later, I look out over my city, and the strong wind on my face reminds me of new beginnings. Suddenly I understand: There's no need to change my name. Instead I will find some way to use my life to help others. Through giving, I will find the strength to face all my challenges. In that moment I think I can still hear it—the wind at Blue Ledges, whispering my Indian name.

Write Definitions

Ten words in the essay are in bold. On a separate sheet of paper, write a definition for each word. Use an English dictionary, or go to dictionary.com. Write your definitions in English.

Summary

In a paragraph of about ten sentences, explain what happened in this essay. Provide answers to the following questions.

• Why was Kline worried and sad at the beginning of the essay?
• When did he go to Camp Flying Cloud?
• What happened at camp?
• What is a naming ceremony?
• How did the memory of his naming ceremony change him?

Writing Topics

Write about one of the following topics. Verify that your essay is well structured by looking at the Essay Checklist on the inside back cover.

1 • Write about your name. You can write about your first name, your last name, and/or your nickname. Think about these questions.

• Who named you?
• Does your name have a meaning?
• Are you named after an ancestor?
• Do you know other people with your name? Who are they?
• How do you feel about your name? Do you like or hate your name? Why?
• When you were younger, what name did you want to have?
• Does your name fit you?

2 • Write about a holiday or celebration that you enjoy.

• Introduce your topic. You can give some background or historical information about the holiday.
• In your first body paragraph, explain what you usually do on that holiday. How does your family celebrate each year?
• In your second body paragraph, describe what you did last year. What did your family do?
• Write a concluding suggestion or prediction.

3 • All cultures celebrate stages of life. They also have religious, political, and national holidays. What do such traditions provide for people?

4 • Each culture has ceremonies to celebrate adulthood. Describe a ceremony that is popular in your culture. Explain it to someone from another culture. For example, you could describe the high school graduation ceremony.

To review some of the vocabulary studied in this chapter, visit the companion website.

*·· People are the same
all over the world. ··*

Anonymous

*·· The world is like a big book. People
who never travel read only one page. ··*

Federico Fellini

Travel
Adventures

Look at the above quotations. How do the quotations contradict each other? Which quotation do you agree with? In this chapter, you will read texts about travelling.

Warm Up ·· Travel Experiences

Work with a partner and discuss how to form each question. Add one of the following auxiliaries to each question: *was, would, do, did,* or *should.* Write your partner's answers below.

Partner's name: _____

1 • What _____ you do every year during your summer vacation?

_____

_____

2 • Where _____ you travel when you were a child?

_____

_____

3 • What _____ the best place that you visited when you were a child?

_____

4 • In the future, where _____ you like to travel? Explain why.

_____

_____

5 • What _____ people bring with them when they travel? List at least five things.

_____

_____

Writing Suggestion

Write a paragraph about your partner.

Tip Grammar

Commonly Confused Travel Words

Travel vs. Trip

- **Travel** is a verb. You **travel** to another place. Do not use it as a noun!
- **Trip** is a noun. You take a **trip** somewhere.

       noun   verb
    I took a **trip** to Jamaica.   I **travelled** to Jamaica.

Vacation vs. Vacancy

- A **vacation** is a break from work or school. You might spend your **vacation** in another place.
- **Vacancy** means "available space." On hotels and motels, you may see a sign saying "No vacancy" to indicate that there are no available rooms.

    On my **vacation**, I went to Spain. The first hotel I visited had no **vacancy**.

Spend vs. Pass

- You **spend** time in a new place.
- You **pass** a test, meaning "you succeed." You also **pass** someone on the road, meaning "you go by them."

    After I **passed** all of my exams, I took a break. I **spent** three weeks in Vancouver.

By vs. Per

- You travel **by** plane, train, bus, or car.
- Use **per** to indicate a quantity or amount completed in a period of time.

    I travelled **by** bus to Halifax. The bus drove at one hundred kilometres **per** hour.

To work on your writing skills, visit the companion website.

Reading

Reading Strategy

Finding Main Ideas

Most essays and stories have a main idea. It may be expressed in the title, or it may appear in the introduction and conclusion of the text.

If you can't find a thesis statement or statement of main idea, ask yourself *who, what, when, where, why,* and *how* questions, and then, in a sentence or two, explain what the text is about. For example, Chapter 5 contains a text called "Naming Good Path Elk." A statement of main idea about that text could be the following:

> In "Naming Good Path Elk," Kenneth Kline describes his experiences during a traditional native naming ceremony, and he explains how the ceremony helped him find his identity.

Reading 6.1

In the next stories, Anthony Wade describes his adventures during his trip to Asia. His stories describe some common mistakes that travellers make. When you read each story, look for main ideas.

Travel Stories
by Anthony Wade

Part 1: Backpacking in Thailand

>>> Thai puppets

1 When I was twenty-one years old, I went on a trip to Asia alone. I wanted to see the world and "find myself." I was confused about my future, and didn't know what to do with my life. I thought that travelling would give me some insight. I had expected to travel for six months, and ended up staying abroad for almost two years.

2 Before going to Thailand I bought a high-quality backpack that was able to hold one hundred pounds of equipment. I filled the backpack with clothing, books, camera equipment, rain gear, a cooking stove, plates, containers, and about four pairs of shoes. I wanted to be prepared for any eventuality.

3 After a few days in Bangkok, I decided to get away from the noise and pollution of the city, so I took a bus south to the islands. At one town along the way, I bought a straw mat and a Thai puppet. Unfortunately, my backpack was full, and I had no room for the souvenirs. I had to carry them in a separate bag.

4 When I arrived on the island of Ko Phan Gan, I made a long journey around a peninsula to get to the travel huts where I would be staying. I walked along the shore for about half an hour. When I finally arrived at the guest huts, I was exhausted, and my back was killing me.

5 I didn't want to carry so many useless items. I emptied my backpack and carefully looked at everything. Then, I made a small pile of things that I would keep. I gave away the rest. I left most of my books at a hotel. I gave my shoes to a local boy. I left clothing on a bench in a nearby village. I also gave away my cooking gear. I don't know what I was thinking! Food in Asia is inexpensive and delicious, so it was crazy to bring along such supplies. I ended up giving away about half of my things. It was really stupid to overpack.

Vocabulary and Comprehension

1• In Paragraph 3, what is a *souvenir*?_____
_____

2• In Paragraph 5, what is the meaning of *overpack*?_____
_____

Are the following sentences true or false? If you answer *false*, then write a true statement.

3• Wade did not give away all of his books.............................T   F
_____

4• Wade needed his cooking supplies..................................T   F
_____

5 • What is the main mistake that Wade made? _____

_____

Part 2: The Japanese Bath

6 After a few weeks in Thailand, I headed to Japan. My most interesting experience there was in a traditional Japanese bathhouse, which is called a *sento*. In the past, both men and women had public baths together, but today the genders bathe separately. There is one section for males and another for females.

7 I visited a public bath in Osaka. I just followed what the other men were doing. In a small room, I took off all of my clothing. Then I entered another room that was filled with men sitting on small stools. Everyone turned to look at me because I was a *gaijin*, or foreigner. I felt a bit embarrassed about being naked.

8 I sat on the stool and, using soap and a cloth, I scrubbed myself clean. I noticed that the other men were taking a long time to scrub, so I kept washing my face and body. Really, I had never spent so much time scrubbing! Then after I was very clean, I grabbed a bucket, and I scooped some water out of the hot tub. I poured the water over myself and rinsed off the dirt and soap. I did exactly what the Japanese men were doing.

9 In Japan, you can only enter a tub when you are completely clean. If you want to wash your hair, you must leave the tub, shampoo, and rinse with the bucket of water. Under no circumstances should you bring soap into the bath.

10 The tubs were quite large, and two or three men were in each tub. The water was extremely hot. While I was soaking, an Australian tourist entered the room, and we introduced ourselves. Then, Kenny just climbed directly into the hot tub, and he brought soap in with him. Everyone else stared at him, shocked.

11 Since he and I were the only ones who spoke English, I told Kenny that he shouldn't bring soap into the tub. He just laughed and said, "Who cares?" He scrubbed his face and arms, and then he rinsed the soap into the water.

12 Kenny complained about the local people and his loud voice really echoed in the room. The other men shook their heads with disgust. I agreed with them. Kenny was a rude and inconsiderate foreigner.

Vocabulary and Comprehension

6 • In Paragraph 7, find a word that means "a seat without arms or a back."

_____

7 • Match the following words with their definitions. To help you choose, look at the word in context. The paragraph number is in parentheses.

TERM		DEFINITION
1. to scrub (8)	_____	a. to let liquid fall from a container
2. to pour (8)	_____	b. to lie in warm water
3. to soak (10)	_____	c. not polite or respectful
4. rude (12)	_____	d. to clean by rubbing vigorously

8 • What should you do in a Japanese bathhouse? List three steps.

_____

_____

_____

9 • What mistakes did Kenny, the Australian tourist, make? Think of at least two things.

_____

_____

Part 3: Visiting India

13 During the last part of my journey, I flew to India. After landing in Delhi, I took trains across the country. India has a fantastic train system with wooden berths that can be lowered to sleep on. Often, in the villages that I visited, there were no Internet cafes. It was also a pain to find public phones. As weeks slid by, I would forget to contact my parents.

14 When I did write home, I mentioned exciting events. For example, in one letter, I described my encounter with a cobra. In Bolpur, a Bengali village, I was staying in a small room with woven straw rafters for the ceiling, and I was sleeping under a mosquito net that was attached to the tall wooden bedposts. In the night, I heard a noise. Looking up, I saw that a cobra had dropped onto my mosquito net! It lay coiled about a foot above my head, suspended in the net. I tried to breathe very slowly and not make a sound. The snake lay curled above me for a few minutes. I was terrified that the netting would break, but luckily, it was strong and it held the weight of the serpent. After a few minutes, the snake uncoiled. I saw the flaps on its neck as it slithered down a bedpost and then moved across the floor. Of course, I didn't sleep that night. In the morning, nobody knew where the cobra had gone. Of course, I left that guest house immediately!

15 I learned, years later, that I had caused my parents a lot of anxiety. During a visit home, my mother explained how worried she and my father had been when I travelled. "When you didn't write, your father would wake up in the night, in a panic, terrified that something bad had happened to you. Sometimes, for weeks, he would express how worried he was. Once, we even considered booking a flight to Asia to try and find you. When one of your letters eventually arrived, we would be comforted for several weeks. But then, a few months later, the panic would begin again. And many of your adventures scared us!"

Vocabulary and Comprehension

10 • In Paragraph 13, what is a *journey*?   **a)** a day   **b)** a trip   **c)** a beginning

11 • In Paragraph 15, what is *booking*? _____

Are the following sentences true or false? If you answer *false*, write a true statement.

12 • The snake bit Wade. .... T   F

_____

13 • In a letter, Wade told his parents about the cobra. .... T   F

_____

14 • When Wade travelled, what two mistakes did he make regarding his parents?

_____

_____

Speaking / Writing ·· International Travel

To read about travel and health, visit the companion website.

Work with a partner. Create a list of suggestions for travellers. To get ideas, think about some of the mistakes that Anthony Wade or Kenny made in "Travel Stories." Explain what travellers should and should not do.

SHOULD DO

_____

_____

_____

_____

_____

SHOULD NOT DO

_____

_____

_____

_____

_____

Project

Create a short brochure explaining what travellers should and should not do. Include photos in your brochure.

Tip Grammar

Using *Should*

When you give advice, you can use the modal auxiliary *should* + the base form of the verb. Avoid the following errors.

- Never add *-s* or *-ed* to the verb that follows *should*.

                    bring
    A traveller **should** not ~~brings~~ too many books.

- Never put *to* between *should* and the verb.

    You **should** ~~to~~ pack carefully.

---

84   PART 3 ·· **CELEBRATIONS AND TRAVEL**

North Korea is a mystery to most people. The secretive country is cut off from the rest of the planet. North Koreans have no contact with the outside world. Are they truly uniform in their thoughts? How do they live their lives? Are they happy? What do they think of Kim Jong Il, the man they must call "Dear Leader"? ABC News correspondent Diane Sawyer takes an unprecedented look at life in Pyongyang, North Korea.

Watching for Vocabulary

Watch the introduction to "Inside North Korea." Fill in the blanks with one of the following words:

entire	twice	picture	mystery
seat	rare	enemy	magazine

1 • Think of it as your ticket to the unknown, your _____ on the plane. And fasten your seat belts. You're heading off to another universe. We have been granted permission for an extremely _____ twelve-day visit to North Korea. It begins in Beijing, China, where we board an old Soviet jet. Destination? Pyongyang, North Korea's capital. On board, in the airline _____, there are headlines about the US which leave no doubt who is public _____ number one. Even the on-board announcement heralds arrival in a state which is also a kind of state of mind.

2 • Kim Jong Il. This is him, the man of _____ and menace, who must be called "the Dear Leader." And above us, at the airport, a _____ of his father, the founder, who is virtually worshipped as a god in this country. Inside the airport, the arrival board says it all. One flight, _____ a week. We are told that only three hundred foreigners are present in this _____ nation of twenty-three million people.

Watching Comprehension

3 • What are *minders* in North Korea?

   a) guides and interpreters   **b)** students   **c)** leaders

4 • What are some things that the Americans could not film?

_____

Are the following sentences true or false?

5 • North Koreans follow Confucian ideals of "loyalty to one's superiors." ...T   F

6 • The mass games in stadiums always involve sports. ....T   F

7 • The people interviewed in the streets strongly support
their government...T   F

8 • What are the main things that Diane Sawyer learned about North Korea?

_____

_____

_____

Written Response

In a paragraph, compare life in North Korea to life in your country.

Reading

Reading 6.2

Andrew Wells decided to take a break from his university studies in Montreal and go travelling. In the next essay, he describes a trip he took down the Grand Canyon.

Pre-Reading Vocabulary

Before reading the essay, learn the following terms. Write the correct letter under the appropriate picture.

| **a)** bighorn sheep | **b)** deer | **c)** ledge | **d)** path | **e)** sole |

_____   _____   _____   _____   _____

The Grand Canyon
by Andrew Wells

1 Twenty years old, on a break from studies, I decided to set out backpacking to see where it would take me. I was in a youth hostel in Flagstaff, Arizona, when I spontaneously decided to see the Grand Canyon. My plan was to hike from the top of the canyon, down to the

Colorado River, and then back up. What I didn't realize was that this sort of hiking is not a simple test of aerobic fitness or personal desire. No, it's a type of brutal self-destruction. The next two days hiking in the canyon left me dazed and **depleted**.

depleted
very tired

2 On the first day, I walked and hitchhiked from Flagstaff and descended eight kilometres before nightfall. I set out the next morning toward the river, and my physical condition rapidly deteriorated. First, the soles of my boots broke and flapped against my feet with every step I took. The blisters on my feet ached continuously. The straps from my backpack tore into my shoulder blades. My focus remained on the path in front of me. I knew that if I lost concentration, at any point I could trip and fall over the edge. At least the awe-inspiring surroundings made it easier to forget the pain.

3 In the canyon, my surroundings were continually changing. At one moment, I was following a winding dirt path under light tree cover, with deer roaming, birds chirping, and small mammals scurrying about. Then suddenly I was on a sandy ledge following a stream that cut between towering walls of red rock. I could see nothing but the three feet in front of me where the wall curved with the stream. Then when I turned a corner, the walls opened up into a majestic gorge that was green and lush. A little farther, as I looked down below me, I could see the trail winding down the gorge and eventually disappearing.

4 Eventually I reached Phantom Ranch at the bottom of the canyon. It serves as a rest stop for **die-hard** hikers and is so popular that people have to reserve years ahead of time. At the ranch I encountered two types of people. There are retired couples who are passionate hikers and who wait two years for reservations. Some that I met had **scaled** Mount Everest. And then there are those who work at the ranch. Most of them don't leave the canyon for months on end because the only way out is a **gruelling** twenty-kilometre trek or a rather expensive ride on the back of a mule. To further their isolation, the media is virtually non-existent. The ranger has a radio, and there's one emergency telephone.

die-hard
determined

scaled
climbed

gruelling
extremely difficult

5 I spoke with the man working the canteen desk. He was a slow talker in his early thirties, tall and thin, with an emotionless expression. While poking at a block of wood with a steel pick, he droned on and on about all the people he knew about who had died in the canyon. "Once, some parents let their three-year old girl walk alone, and she just walked right off the edge. Another time a couple tried to hike in from the far west, ran out of water, and expired." He kept tapping the wood with his pick. "Then there was the guy who was **knocked off** the edge by one of the sheep." In my head I screamed, "Stop! Please stop!"

knocked off
pushed off

6 If a hiker is tired at the bottom of the canyon, he's in serious trouble. Trouble was what I came face-to-face with. Climbing back up, I encountered a

bighorn sheep on a narrow ledge. It wanted to go where I was, and I wanted to go where it was, but there was no room to pass. For minutes on end the sheep and I engaged in a stare-down. Then all of a sudden it got bored with me and climbed up an 85-degree sheer rock face! I was **dumbfounded**. It was so smart, and as soon as I passed, it climbed back down, turned and looked at me, and walked on. It understood perfectly what was going on.

dumbfounded
shocked

7 After several hours of non-stop hiking, I had absolutely no energy left. The rock face kept getting **steeper** and the air significantly thinner. Each layer of the canyon above me was hidden behind the nearest wall of towering sandstone. So when I thought I had gotten to the top, to my great **dismay**, a whole new area opened up above me. Then a woman in at least her late seventies **plowed** past me on her way uphill out of the canyon. She was no more than five feet tall. I was honestly in pretty good hiking shape. I passed just about everyone else, but this woman was unbelievable. (I was carrying a twenty-pound pack though, so I want a rematch.)

steeper
closer to being perpendicular

dismay
consternation

plowed
walked quickly

8 At certain points I felt like saying, "That's it. I'm living the rest of my life on this ledge. I'm not moving." And then I started making deals with myself, planning what I was going to do with my life once I got out, just to motivate myself to keep going. When I reached the top, I looked down into the **bowels** of the canyon and felt relieved that I had done it. It's something that does not need to be done more than once. I can retain the knowledge of what I have accomplished. I have come out believing that there's nothing that can stop me, and there's no greater feeling.

bowels
lowest parts

Write Questions

Imagine that you are a reporter who must interview Andrew Wells. On a separate piece of paper, compose ten questions that you would like to ask him. Use at least two verb tenses in your questions. Remember to use the proper word order.

 Tip Grammar

Question Form

Ensure that your questions have the proper word order.

Question word	+	Auxiliary	+	Subject	+	Verb	+	Rest of sentence
Why		did		you		go		to the Grand Canyon?

 **Speaking / Writing** ·· Tourism Project

Part 1: Vocabulary

With a partner, match the words that are in bold with their correct definitions.

© Pearson Longman – Reproduction prohibited

TERM		DEFINITION
1. a **round-trip** ticket	_____	a. enter; go into
2. the planes **take off**	_____	b. air host(ess); steward(ess)
3. the planes **land**	_____	c. leave the runway and fly into the air
4. **book** a ticket	_____	d. official at an international border who checks your luggage and passport
5. **luggage**	_____	e. arrive on the runway from the air
6. **board** the plane	_____	f. reserve
7. **flight attendant**	_____	g. ticket to a destination and back home
8. **customs officer**	_____	h. baggage

Part 2: Project

With your partner, choose one of the following regions of the world. Then choose a country. Finally, choose a major tourist area in that country.

South America	Caribbean	North America	Africa
Asia	Europe	Middle East	Australia

Using the Internet, do some research. Then make a poster that you will present to a group of classmates. Your presentation should include most of the following information.

- **Location:** Use a map or globe to explain where the country and major cities are located.
- **Cost:** What is the best price for plane tickets to that location?
- **Currency:** What kind of currency will people need? What is the exchange rate?
- **Accommodations:** Where can a student stay? Find an economic hotel or youth hostel.
- **Attractions:** Explain some things that visitors can do in the region. Bring photos to show those attractions.
- **Precautions:** What should travellers to the region know? Do they need vaccinations? Should they take special precautions?

> **Tip**
>
> Presentation
> - Prepare! Time yourself. Each person in your team must speak for at least two minutes. Because your presentation is short, focus on main points.
> - Use your own words. If you get information from a site, ensure that you restate it in your own words.
> - Bring visuals. You should bring pictures of the location. You can put the pictures on your poster. You can find pictures on the Internet.
> - Do not read. Use cue cards. (Choose key words from your presentation.)
> - After other students make their presentations, you must ask those students questions. Before your presentation date, review how to form questions.

To practise your speaking skills, visit the companion website.

 **Listening**

Follow Directions

Listen carefully to the directions. Indicate where each place appears on the map.

drugstore	barber shop	bakery	antique shop	video store	home

CHURCH

LAUNDROMAT

LUKA'S FASHIONS

HARRY'S HARDWARE

DOUGHNUT SHOP

ADSO BANK

2nd AVENUE

GIBSON STREET

PILO'S GROCERIES

PARKING

SPORTS CENTRE

MARLON'S COMPUTERS

LOIS LANE

ICE CREAM SHOP

1st AVENUE

PADLEY PARK

2nd AVENUE

FIRST PIZZA

Austria
China
England
Finland
France
Germany
India
Ireland
Italy
Malaysia
Netherlands
Portugal
Russia
Saudi Arabia
Scotland
Spain
Switzerland
Turkey

Identify Countries

The speaker will talk about different countries. Write the name of the correct country in the space provided.

Choose from the countries listed on the left.

1. _____   6. _____

2. _____   7. _____

3. _____   8. _____

4. _____   9. _____

5. _____   10. _____

Listening A Traveller's Story

Eva Burns travelled to Europe. In the listening segment, Eva discusses her European vacation.

Listening Comprehension

Part 1: Listen for the Itinerary

Eva visited six countries on her European trip. On the following map, put a number on the countries in the order that she visited them.

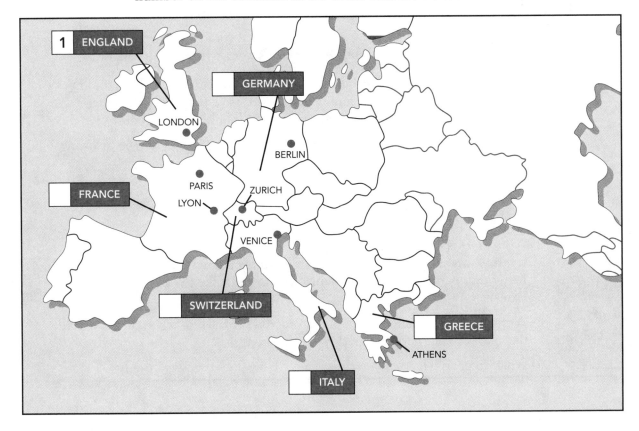

Part 2: Listen for Details

1 • When did Eva leave home?   **a)** in January   **b)** in May   **c)** in June

2 • Why does Eva like to travel alone?

_____

3 • What is a youth hostel? _____

4 • What was Eva's favourite country in Europe? _____

5 • Did Eva's parents give Eva money for her trip?   Yes ☐   No ☐

6 • Name two European countries where Eva found a job.

_____   _____

7 • What two jobs did Eva do? _____

_____

8 • Eva gives advice to travellers. What advice does she give?

_____

9 • Eva said that travelling changed her life. How did it change her life?

_____

Writing Topics

Write about one of the following topics. Verify that your essay is well structured by looking at the Essay Checklist on the inside back cover.

1 • Describe your family's travel history. If your family came here from another country, explain where your family originated. How did your family get here? How is this country different from your family's native country?

2 • Describe your culture to someone from another country. Include the following information:
   • What food is special to your culture?
   • What are some traditions or celebrations?
   • What should visitors to your region know?

3 • Write an essay about travelling. In one paragraph, describe some trips that you took when you were younger. Where did you go? What did you do? In another paragraph, describe a place you would like to visit in the future. Explain why.

4 • Write an essay explaining how people should prepare for a trip. What should they pack? What information do they need?

5 • What do people learn when they travel? How does it change them?

To review some of the vocabulary studied in this chapter, visit the companion website.

*•• Don't judge a book
by its cover. ••*

Proverb

Life Experiences

In this chapter, you will read about some people who had life-changing experiences.

Warm Up •• Proverbs and Wise Sayings

With a partner or a small group of students, look at each of the following proverbs. If a proverb's meaning is not clear, discuss possible interpretations with your group or with your teacher, and rewrite the proverb.

Example: Blood is thicker than water. _____*Family is very important.*_____

1• Don't throw out the baby with the bathwater.

_____

2• Where there is smoke, there is fire.

_____

3• Practise what you preach.

_____

4• Don't put all your eggs in one basket.

_____

5• Look before you leap.

_____

6• The grass always looks greener on the other side of the fence.

_____

7• Don't bite the hand that feeds you.

_____

8• Beauty is skin deep.

_____

9• The average person thinks he isn't.

_____

10• A bird in the hand is worth two in a bush.

_____

To work on your writing skills, visit the companion website.

Reading

Reading Strategy

Finding the Message

Sometimes, the meaning of a reading is not immediately clear. You must search for the author's message by reading between the lines. In other words, look for clues in the text, and use your logic to make a guess about the author's meaning.

Reading Exercise

Read the following paragraph. Guess what the author is trying to say.

> A young man named Jerome loved to play poker with his friends. Whenever he won a game, Jerome laughed with happiness. But Jerome hated to lose, and when he lost a game, he became angry and abusive to his friends. One by one, his friends refused to play cards with him. Within six months, Jerome no longer had card-playing partners.

What is the message? (There may be more than one message.)

_____

_____

Pair Reading Activity (Optional)

Find a partner. One of you can read "Sports and Life" and the other can read "School Lessons."

Answer the questions that follow your reading. Later, you will share information with your partner.

Reading 7.1

In the following essay, Jeff Kemp recounts what happened during his early years as a professional football player. When you finish reading, think about the message.

Sports and Life
by Jeff Kemp

1 We live in an age when, too often, rules are scorned, values are turned upside down, principles are replaced by **expediency**, and character is sacrificed for popularity. Individual athletes are sometimes the worst offenders, but not as often as one might think. In fact, sports teach important moral lessons that athletes can apply on and off the playing field.

expediency
convenience

2   Many people dream of being a professional athlete. For me, the dream seemed to be within reach because my father, Jack Kemp, an outstanding quarterback, played for the American Football League's Buffalo Bills (prior to the AFL's 1970 merger with the National Football League). The trouble was, I was not very good! I was a third-string football player through most of junior high and high school and for two years at Dartmouth College. I was not anyone's idea of a "hot prospect." After graduation, I was **passed over** by NFL scouts. When I finally was asked to join the Los Angeles Rams in 1981 as a free agent, I was **designated** as fifth-string quarterback.

passed over
not chosen

designated
selected

3   It was a fifty-to-one shot that I would survive training camp. Rookies were the only players required to show up for the first week of camp. There were dozens competing for the few spots open on the team. After two days, a young boy approached me as I was walking off the field. He asked if he could carry my helmet to the locker room. It was a long way, but I said, "Sure, I think you can handle that." The next morning, he showed up before practice and offered to carry my helmet and shoulder pads, and he was there again after practice offering the same service. So it went for the rest of the week.

4   On the last day, as we were departing the field, my young assistant said, "Jeff, can I ask you a question?" (We were on a first-name basis by then.)

5   I thought, "This is my first fan! He is going to ask me for an autograph."

6   He then inquired, "When do the good football players come to camp?" Right then and there, I learned a lesson in humility from a seven-year-old boy.

7   In my first three NFL seasons, I was forced to learn the same lesson over and over again. During that time, I threw just thirty-one passes. Nevertheless, by 1984, I had managed to outlast the five NFL quarterbacks who had been ahead of me. With the Rams' record standing at 1-2, I took over for injured quarterback Vince Ferragamo and earned my first start against the Cincinnati Bengals, eventually leading the Rams to nine more victories and a playoff berth.

8   The next season, I returned to the bench as a backup quarterback. Humility, I was compelled to remind myself, was a good thing. It helped me appreciate what I had and avoid dwelling on what I did not have. It prevented complaining, which drains the spirit and unity of any group. It also led me to persevere and be ready whenever opportunity presented itself.

>>> Football and helmet

Vocabulary

1 • Find a word in Paragraph 2 that means "fantastic." _____

2 • In Paragraph 3, what is the meaning of *rookie*?

    a) veteran; experienced player   **b)** inexperienced player

3 • Find a word in Paragraph 7 that means "to survive longer than the others."

_____

4 • Find a word in Paragraph 8 that means "thinking about or worrying about obsessively."

_____

Comprehension

5 • What happened to Jeff Kemp? Use your own words to describe the events.

_____

_____

_____

_____

_____

_____

6 • What did Kemp learn?

_____

_____

_____

7 • Which proverb from the chapter's Warm Up would best sum up the lesson in this essay?

_____

Reading 7.2

Most people make mistakes during their childhood. In the next essay, Andrea Zedrick discusses lessons she learned in school.

School Lessons
by Andrea Zedrick

1   The German author Johann Wolfgang Goethe once said, "Everyone believes in his youth that the world really began with him and that everything exists for his benefit." I feel **ashamed** when I remember the following incidents in my youth. My only solace is the realization that my mistakes helped me become a better person.

[handwritten notes: quand qu'on ai jeune on pense que le monde tourne autour de nous ses erreurs]

ashamed embarrassed and guilty *[handwritten: j'ai aider a devenir une meilleur personne]*

2 I was a very superficial kid. In Grade 6, when an overweight girl named Jackie joined our class, I made fun of her. Like my classmates, I picked "Jackie **fleas**" off her back and called her "the tank." One afternoon, as I was walking home, I saw Jackie ahead of me. She was crying. Then, a few days later, she suddenly stopped coming to school.

3 A few weeks passed. Our teacher told us that Jackie was in the hospital but he didn't explain why. We gossiped about our classmate. Some said Jackie had a serious illness, and others claimed that she had tried to kill herself. She never returned to our school after that.

4 For a while, I felt guilty and wished that I had been nicer to Jackie. But honestly, I soon forgot her. I was still obsessed with appearances, and I wanted to associate with popular people. The next fall, when I entered Grade 7, I had two good friends at school, but I longed to hang out with the kids in the "cool" gang. They wore $150 sneakers and expensive brand-name clothing.

5 I manipulated my mother until she bought me Nike running shoes. I did the same thing when designer jeans became popular, when "Tommy" sweaters were fashionable, and then when feather-filled ski jackets became the rage. My mother was raising me by herself. She worked as a receptionist in a dentist's office and her salary wasn't very high, but I didn't care. My mother was easy to manipulate and she always caved in to my demands.

6 One afternoon, when I came home and found my mother gluing back the heel on her shoes, I realized how selfish I had been. I also had to admit that the popular kids were ignoring me even when I wore designer jeans. I decided to buy used clothing in thrift shops. I also decided to appreciate my real friends.

7 When I was twenty, I met Jackie, the girl from the sixth grade, at a party. She had lost a lot of weight, and she was entertaining a crowd with her sense of humour. When I had the chance, I apologized for being such a superficial little brat in school. "I've really changed," I insisted, as she looked at me skeptically.

8 I can't pretend that I completely stopped caring about appearances, but I did learn to look below the surface. I now know that the most beautiful people are those who know how to listen and can make others smile.

9 I made other mistakes during those years. I took some stupid risks and exercised poor judgment. Perhaps by writing about that period of my life, I am hoping for some type of absolution. You know, maybe others will learn from my mistakes. But that is the problem with mistakes: we only truly learn from them when we make them ourselves.

Vocabulary

1 • In Paragraph 2, the writer says, "I made fun of her." What is the meaning of *made fun of*?

   a) ridiculed   **b)** had a fun, happy time   **c)** ignored

2 • Find a verb in Paragraph 3 that means "talked about someone without her knowledge."

_____

3 • Find a two-word expression in Paragraph 5 that means "reluctantly agreed."

_____

4 • In Paragraph 6, what is the meaning of *selfish*?

   a) happy   **b)** angry   **c)** egotistical and self-centred

Comprehension

5 • What happened to Andrea Zedrick? Use your own words to describe the main events.

_____

_____

_____

_____

_____

_____

6 • Using your own words, describe what Zedrick learned.

_____

_____

_____

7 • Which proverb from the chapter's Warm Up would best sum up the lesson in this essay?

_____

Pair Reading •• Share Information

> **Tip Grammar**
>
> *His* or *Her*?
> Possessive adjectives agree with the possessor, not with the object that is possessed. Therefore, when something belongs to a male, use *his* + noun.
> When something belongs to a female, use *her* + noun.
>
>   Jeff was surprised when the boy asked to carry **his** helmet.
>
>   Andrea asked **her** mother for expensive clothing.

1• Work with the student who has read the other reading. Match each term with its definition.

TERM		DEFINITION
1. outstanding	_____	a. to survive longer than the others
2. to make fun of	_____	b. to think about something obsessively
3. to gossip	_____	c. fantastic
4. to outlast	_____	d. to surrender; to agree
5. to cave in	_____	e. to talk about people without their knowledge
6. to dwell	_____	f. to ridicule

2• Compare the experiences of Jeff Kemp with those of Andrea Zedrick. Write down information in the chart. You do not have to write complete sentences.

	JEFF KEMP	ANDREA ZEDRICK
What happened?		
What lesson did he or she learn? What was the message?		

3• A male wrote "Sports and Life," and a female wrote "School Lessons." Think about the differences in the essays. What pressures do males face? What pressures do females face? Are the pressures the same?

MALES	FEMALES
_____	_____
_____	_____
_____	_____

To develop your listening skills, visit the companion website.

Speaking ·· Truth or Lie

Write three sentences about yourself. Make two false sentences and one true sentence. Remember, two of your sentences are not true. One of your sentences is true.

Write your three sentences on a piece of heavy paper or cardboard because you will show them to teammates. Then your teammates will ask you questions to discover which story is true. After students ask questions, you must give a two-minute presentation about the true story. In your presentation, give general information and some details about your story.

Example: Pierre says,

I won a tennis tournament when I was fifteen.   (This is not true.)

I take singing lessons.   (This is not true.)

I went to Florida in 1995.   (This is true.)

After his team guesses the true story, Pierre talks about the true story for about two minutes.

To perfect your reading skills, visit the companion website.

 Tip

Presentation

- You can use notes or cue cards with main words. Do not read!
- Practise your presentation.
- If possible, bring in something visual about your true story. It could be a photo or an object.
- Use at least two verb tenses in your story.

 **Listening**

Listen to Specific Words

You will hear one word from each word pair. The word will be repeated. Underline the word that you hear.

Example: <u>is</u> his

1. it	hit	6. hear	ear	11. is	his
2. hat	at	7. ate	hate	12. can	can't
3. hand	and	8. harm	arm	13. should	shouldn't
4. hair	air	9. his	he's	14. tank	thank
5. old	hold	10. her	hers	15. taught	thought

Listen to Sentences

Listen to each sentence and underline the word that you hear. Listen carefully to word endings.

1. Last (Tuesday / Thursday), Clayton Chen had an accident. The fourteen (year / years) old boy was riding a moped, and he went through a stop (sign / signs). A car (hit / hits) him. Unfortunately, Clayton (hurt / hurts) his arm. Also, the car damaged (is / his) moped.

2. Now, Clayton is at home. He (can / can't) go to school, but his mother is keeping him home for a few (day / days) anyway. She (want / wants) him to wait until he (feel / feels) better. He (spend / spends) his time in front of the television. Anyway, even if he went to school, he (could / couldn't) write very well because he broke his right arm.

3. Clayton (can / can't) understand how the accident happened. He (can / can't) remember the details very well. Usually, he (can / can't) see if a car is coming, and then he (stop / stops) in time.

Listening My Mistake

Everyone makes mistakes. Sometimes, if we are lucky, we can learn from our errors. A young man named David describes what happened to him. Listen carefully.

Pre-Listening Vocabulary

Match each term with its correct meaning. Write the letter of the appropriate definition in the space provided.

TERM		DEFINITION
1. driver's licence	_____	a. cement blocks that separate two parts of a road
2. part-time job	_____	b. to drive very quickly
3. to race	_____	c. to move from one "track" to another on a road
4. to speed	_____	d. legal permit to drive a car
5. to change lanes	_____	e. a job that is only a few days a week
6. concrete divider	_____	f. to compete to see who is the fastest

Take Notes

Listen to the tape and take careful notes. List what happens. (Don't write complete sentences; just write down key words and phrases.)

• *David - driver's licence - sixteen years old* _____

• _____

• _____

• _____

• _____

• _____

• _____

• _____

• _____

• _____

Write a Summary

Now summarize what happened to Alex. On a separate sheet, write seven to ten sentences. Explain where Alex was, what happened, and what he learned. Use the past tense.

> ### Tip Grammar
>
> **Negative Past Tense Forms**
>
> Use the correct past tense verbs. There is a list of common irregular verbs in *Open Book Grammar*. To make past tense verbs negative, add the auxiliary *did not* to the verb. Do not use the past form of the main verb!
>
> tell
>
> He **did not** ~~told~~ the truth.
>
> When the verb is *be*, just add *not*.
>
> They **were not** nice to each other.

Reading

Reading 7.3

In his memoir, *Cockeyed*, Ryan Knighton, a Vancouver-based author and teacher, describes his slow descent into blindness. The following essay examines Knighton's frustrating experience with language.

Out of Sight
by Ryan Knighton

1 On my eighteenth birthday, my first retina specialist, a man who delivered his bedside manner like napalm, informed me that I would be blind within a few years. No cure, he said, sorry. The specialist told me the name of the condition, *retinitis pigmentosa*. He described how it would soon **eradicate** my remaining night vision, limit me to tunnel vision, and eventually **blinker** me altogether. The whole scene took less than ten minutes.

eradicate
remove completely

blinker
blind

2 For four years, I had exhibited clumsy behaviour nobody could account for. As a **warehouse** worker during summer vacations, I drove a forklift and ran over nearly everything possible, including one of my co-workers. True, I hated him and his insistence that we play nothing but Iron Maiden on the shipping area stereo, but it wasn't in my character to crush him.

warehouse
a place to store products; entrepôt

3 But the real giveaway came when I drove my father's Pontiac into a **ditch**. Lots of friends crashed their parents' cars, but my accident stood out. I did my teenaged duty at roughly five kilometres per hour. How do you miss a turn at that speed unless your eyes are closed? After sundown, mine might as well have been.

ditch
trench at the side of a road

4 When I reported to my mother that, as a new driver, I was having trouble on rainy nights, she said they gave everybody trouble and told me not to worry. I was on my way out the door, about to drive to work. "But do you use the cat's eyes sometimes?" I asked.

5 "Sure," she said. "That's what they're for, reflecting light when it's hard to see the yellow line."

6 "No, I mean do you use them, do you drive on them?"

7 When I couldn't see the yellow line, I had taken to steering onto the cat's eyes. This, I found, helped position me on the road. I was a little close to the middle, maybe, but better than anything I could determine on my own. The *clunk clunk clunk* of the reflectors under my tires let me know where I was. I suppose I drove Braille.

8 "You drive on the cat's eyes?" my mother asked.

9 "Well, only at night." I would wager my mother called for my first ophthal-mological appointment by the time I had shut the front door behind me.

10 Retinitis pigmentosa is the loss of photoreceptors associated with pigmentary changes in the retina. Another way to put it is that my retina is **scarring** itself to death. I've enjoyed the slow loss of all peripheral and night vision. By my own estimate, I have a year to go until that tiny pinhole of clarity in which I live will consume itself, and the lights will go out. To know what's filling up my little tunnel, I rely mostly on context.

scarring
becoming thick and opaque

11 Once I asked a red-headed waitress for directions to the washroom. I didn't know she was a waitress by the colour of her hair, of course —the bit of it I saw—but by the smell of coffee, which was quickly overwhelmed by a perfumy fog.

12 "Would you like more coffee?"

13 "I'd love coffee," I said, "but I'd love to be in your washroom even more."

14 "Um, okay, the men's room is over that way."

15 I stared vacantly ahead while she, I imagine, continued to point "that way." Then I heard the pleasant sound of coffee being poured.

16 "I'm sorry," I said, "but I don't know what *that way* means." I plucked my white cane from the bag beside me. "I guess it wasn't obvious, and I forgot to—"

17 "Oh my God, I'm sorry, I didn't know you're blind! You didn't look—you don't look—not at all—I mean really."

18 I smiled with that warm sensation you get when you are sixteen and someone says you look like you're in your twenties. "Thanks, that is very kind. Where did you say the washroom is?"

19 "At the back."

20 "Which way is back?"

21 "It's over there," she said, and walked away.

22 All I wanted were specific directions. Instead, my waitress gave me a demonstration of the fact that, along with vision, parts of language disappear into blindness. The capacity of language to guide me has atrophied. Not even Braille can substitute for some words. *This way. Right here, in front of you. No, there. Right there, under your nose.* Such directional cues have lost their meaning. Who would have guessed that a disease can alter language as it alters the body, disabling parts of speech—that language is, in this way, an extension of the body and subject to the same pathologies.

23 "EXCUSE ME."

24 My waitress was back, not a second too soon. I really did need to use the facilities.

25 "I don't mean to intrude," she said, "but didn't you go to Langley Secondary School?"

26 "Yes, I did."

27 "It's Ryan, right? I'm Danielle! We were in drama class together. God, I didn't recognize you at all. You look so different now," she said.

28 I braced myself. "I'm not sure what it is. Maybe it's—" *The fierce squint? The white cane? The expression of perpetual disorientation?*

29 "It's—well. I know!" She put a hand on my head with daring compassion. "You shaved your hair off. When did you do that?"

30 Now I was free to burn with embarrassment at my self-centredness. Just because it's a sighted world doesn't mean blindness is the first thing people notice about me, nor the first thing that comes to mind. Along with mutant celebrity and meaningless words, I suppose paranoia is another side effect. "A couple of years ago, I guess," I replied.

31 "Looks cool."

32 "Thanks."

33 "I remember in high school your hair used to be long," she said. "Really long. It was down to here, right?"

Vocabulary and Comprehension

Write your answers in the spaces provided. *Do not use a dictionary.* Guess the meanings of words by using context clues.

1• Find a word in Paragraph 2 that means "uncoordinated, awkward."

_____

2 • In Paragraph 2, what is a *forklift*? Use your logic when you make a guess.

a) an eating utensil

b) a large wooden box

c) a vehicle that can lift heavy objects

3 • In Paragraph 4, what are *cat's eyes*? Look for context clues in the surrounding paragraphs.

a) raised white reflectors that show the line on a road

b) a car's headlights, or front lights, when they are in the high position

c) the lines in a person's eyes

4 • Look in Paragraphs 15 to 18. Find a verb that means "took or removed."

_____

5 • Find a word in Paragraph 22 that means "change or modify."

_____

6 • In Paragraph 1, Knighton's doctor was

a) very compassionate and gentle

b) very direct and brusque

c) sympathetic

d) purposely cruel

7 • What is not true about Paragraph 2?

a) Knighton planned to damage his co-worker.

b) Knighton ran over his co-worker with a forklift.

c) Knighton's co-worker liked listening to the rock band Iron Maiden.

d) Knighton did not like the music of Iron Maiden.

8 • What signs or indications showed that Knighton might be losing his vision?

a) He kept hitting things and running over things at work.

b) He drove on the cat's eyes.

c) He had an accident while he was driving.

d) All of the answers

9 • When he wrote this essay, how well could the author see?

a) He was completely blind. He could see nothing.

b) He could see the edges. In other words, he had peripheral vision.

c) He could see a very small amount in the centre of his vision.

10 • In the events of Paragraphs 11 to 19, which came last?

   a) He asked for directions to the washroom.

   b) The waitress realized that her customer was blind.

   c) He showed his white cane to the waitress.

   d) He asked for coffee.

11 • What is the main idea of Paragraph 22?

   a) The author cannot see.

   b) Language is an extension of his body.

   c) When a person becomes blind, many words lose their meaning.

   d) The waitress cannot give directions.

12 • How did the waitress first meet Knighton?

   a) They met in high school.

   b) They met in the restaurant.

   c) They met at a party.

   d) They met at the warehouse.

13 • Reread Paragraphs 25 to 30. What is the author's main message in those paragraphs?

   a) He went to Langley Secondary School.

   b) He was in drama class with Danielle.

   c) He felt embarrassed when he realized that Danielle was an old classmate.

   d) He realized that his blindness is not the first thing people see when they meet him.

14 • What is the significance of the last paragraph (Paragraph 33)?

   a) Knighton had long hair many years before.

   b) The waitress continued to use words that the author would not understand.

   c) The waitress liked Knighton.

   d) The waitress had long hair.

15 • What is the main idea of this essay? (The main idea is *not* the message. To find the main idea, think how you would sum up this essay to another person.)

   a) Life is cruel.

   b) Ryan Knighton describes his visit to a restaurant and explains how his loss of vision has also made some words meaningless.

   c) Ryan Knighton has old friends from high school, and sometimes he meets those friends in public places.

   d) One day, Ryan Knighton went to his doctor's office, and he learned that he was losing his vision.

Watching •• The Big Snit

This award-winning animated film looks at two simultaneous conflicts. It presents an important lesson.

Pre-Watching Vocabulary

Discuss the following terms with your classmates. Use your dictionary to define the words, if necessary.

Scrabble game	to shake	a saw	letters	a birdcage

Watching Comprehension

Now watch the short film and answer the following questions.

1• What are the the man and the woman doing at the beginning of the film?

_____

2• Why does the woman leave the room?

_____

3• Why does the man begin to use a saw?

_____

4• While the man is taking a nap, the cat bites on the TV cord. What was on television?

_____

5• Why does the couple start to fight?

_____

_____

6• What events help to make the couple stop fighting?

_____

_____

7• How does the video end?

_____

_____

8• What is the message in the video?

_____

_____

Written Response

Write a paragraph describing what happens in the video. Your paragraph should be about 80 to 100 words. Use the present tenses.

Example: A man and woman are playing Scrabble. Suddenly…

 **Speaking** ·· Modern Fables

Each year, many tragic or happy events appear in the newspapers. These events contain one or more lessons for all of us. Discuss the following event with a partner and decide what lessons we can learn.

> A poor family from Quebec, Canada, won $7.6 million in lottery. The Lavigueurs lived in a small apartment before they won the lottery. One of the Lavigueur daughters, seventeen-year-old Louise, did not contribute to the purchase of the lottery ticket, so her family decided that she could not share in the winnings. She took her own family to court. In the meantime, the rest of the family bought a huge and expensive mansion. Five years later, the Lavigueur son developed a drug problem and Louise died from a heart attack. A few years later, the father died. Now the money is gone, and the remaining family members no longer live extravagantly.

What lessons can we learn from this story?

_____

_____

Presentation

Present a life lesson. You can do one of the following:

1• Find a story in the news. Explain what happened. What lesson can we learn from this story?

2• Talk about a mistake that you (or someone you know) made. Explain what happened. What can we learn from your story?

 Tip

Presentation
- Begin your presentation with a short introduction.
- You can use notes or cue cards with main words. Do not read!
- Practise your presentation.
- Make sure that your verb tenses are correct.

 **Writing Topics**

Choose one of the following topics and write an essay. Your essay should have a short introduction.

1• Compare high school life with college or university life. First, describe high school schedules, teachers, or classes. How is college life different from high school life?

2• What do we really learn in high school? Write an essay about some things that you learned during your high school years. In your last paragraph, explain how you are different today.

3• Describe an event that changed your life. What happened? What did you learn?

To review some of the vocabulary studied in this chapter, visit the companion website.

•• Forbidden fruit is the sweetest. ••

English proverb

Legal Limits

Every society has a series of shared rules that are legally enforced. Are some laws unjust? Why do people break laws? This chapter examines our legal limits.

Warm Up •• Crimes

Part 1

Match the crimes with the descriptions. Write the letter of the correct description in the space beside each crime term.

CRIME		DESCRIPTION
1. to jaywalk	_____	a. to drive faster than the speed limit
2. to hit and run	_____	b. an accidental killing
3. to assault	_____	c. to abduct and confine another person
4. manslaughter	_____	d. to illegally cross the street against a traffic light or between marked crosswalks
5. to commit fraud	_____	e. to crash a car into someone and then drive away
6. to kidnap	_____	f. to bring contraband items over international borders
7. to shoplift	_____	g. to intentionally set a fire
8. to smuggle	_____	h. to physically attack someone
9. to speed	_____	i. to steal items from a store
10. to commit arson	_____	j. to create false documents or write bad cheques

Part 2

Answer the following questions with a partner or group of students.

To practice your speaking skills, visit the companion website.

1• In the list in Part 1, which three crimes are the most serious?

_____ _____ _____

2• Which three crimes are least serious?

_____ _____ _____

Reading

Reading Strategy

Scanning

Scanning means "to read quickly to find specific information." For example, when you want to find a phone number, you scan the phone book. You also scan library books or Internet articles to see if they have information that you need. Your eye searches for key words or phrases. (Note: *scan* has other meanings. For example, a computer scanner scans, or reproduces, an image for use as a computer file.)

Reading Exercise

Scan this workbook.

1 • When was this book published? _____

2 • On what page is the text "Frida: Mexico's Passion"? _____

3 • How many chapters does this book have? _____

4 • On what page is the watching activity Second Life? _____

5 • Which chapter contains a list of proverbs? _____

6 • Which page contains information about writing an introduction? _____

Reading 8.1

Answer the questions that follow this reading. You will need to scan the information about crime rates in Canada.

Crime Rates in Canada

1 The crime rate decreased 5% in 2005, primarily fuelled by non-violent crimes (Figure 1). Property crimes decreased by 6%, while other Criminal Code offences dropped by 5%. The rate of violent crime remained stable, despite higher counts of homicides and attempted murders.

2 The national crime rate had increased during the 1960s, '70s, and '80s, peaking in 1991. Crime rates then fell throughout the rest of the 1990s, stabilizing somewhat in the early 2000s. In 2005, the overall crime rate was similar to the rate in 2002.

3 Every province and territory contributed to the drop in 2005. The largest decreases among the provinces were found in Manitoba (–8%), New Brunswick (–8%) and Saskatchewan (–6%).

Figure 1

Crime rate peaked in 1991

Rate per 100,000 population

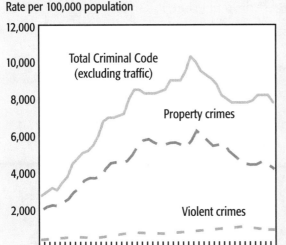

Figure 2

Quebec and Ontario have lowest crime rates, 2005

Rate per 100,000 population

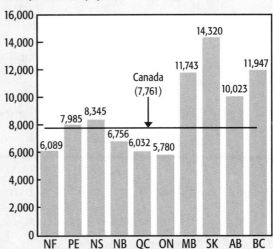

Source: Statistics Canada, Canadian Centre for Justice Statistics, Uniform Crime Reporting Survey

Crime Rates Vary across the Country

4 There are substantial regional differences in crime rates. Prior to 2002, crime rates historically increased from east to west. However, in recent years, Ontario and Quebec recorded lower rates than most Atlantic provinces. This was further reinforced in 2005, as Ontario and Quebec recorded rates that were lower than *all* Atlantic provinces (Figure 2). The western provinces continued to have the highest rates among the provinces and, consistent with previous years, rates in the three territories far surpassed those recorded by the provinces. It should be noted that crime rates in the territories can have large year-over-year fluctuations due to their relatively small populations.

5 Provincial crime rates varied from a low of 5,780 incidents per 100,000 population in Ontario to a high of 14,320 in Saskatchewan. Among the Atlantic provinces, Newfoundland and Labrador had the lowest recorded crime rate for the twenty-second consecutive year, while for the western provinces, Alberta had the lowest rate for the thirteenth straight year.

Crimes Rates in the Territories

6 While the actual number of criminal incidents is relatively low in the Territories, when calculated as a rate per 100,000 population, the overall crime rate is substantially higher compared to the provinces. This has been the case historically.

7 In 2005, the crime rates in the three Territories ranged from three times higher than the national average in the Yukon to five times higher in the Northwest Territories. Despite having much higher rates for total violent crimes, robbery rates in the Territories were among the lowest in the country, with rates that were comparable to those in the Atlantic provinces. In addition, the overall rates of property crime in the Territories were only slightly higher than the rates recorded by the western provinces.

Scanning

Scan the text "Crime Rates in Canada."

1 • Which two provinces had the largest drop in crime in 2005?

_____   _____

2 • Which two provinces had the lowest crime rate in 2005?

_____   _____

3 • Which crimes are more common?

a) property crimes   **b)** violent crimes

4 • Prior to 2002, crimes increased

a) from east to west.   **b)** from west to east.

5 • Which area of Canada has the highest crime rate?

a) western provinces   **b)** eastern provinces   **c)** Northwest Territories

6 • Which three provinces had the highest crime rate in 2005?

_____   _____   _____

7 • Between 1962 and 2005, in what year did the national crime rate peak
(reach its highest point)? _____

Reading 8.2

The following essay looks at traffic laws that are often broken.

Breaking Traffic Laws

1 Governments make laws, and police officers enforce them. Ask most people, and they will insist they are law-abiding. Dig a little deeper, though, and the hidden criminal emerges. In fact, most of us are lawbreakers.

2 Many honest citizens break traffic rules when they go walking. Armando Guzman, a Montreal exterminator, says that he respects the law, yet when I walked with him through downtown Montreal, the truth became evident. Guzman is an unapologetic jaywalker. He refuses to stand on the curb waiting for the light to change when there is no traffic in sight. He also crosses between intersections rather than make the long walk to the corner. "It is ridiculous to wait when I know I can cross safely," Guzman argues.

3 Why are people lawbreakers? Some citizens break laws that they disagree with. Martin Sahr, a Vancouver resident, regularly drives without a seatbelt, an unlawful act that can result in a fine. In 2006, Sahr received a $120 fine for failing to buckle up. He says indignantly, "If I want to risk my life by driving without a seatbelt, it's nobody's business but my own."

4 The locked-door law makes motorists particularly cranky. Pierre Lemay drives a fifteen-year-old Honda to the train station near his home in Boisbriand. Until recently, his unlocked car would sit in the station parking lot while Lemay worked in the city. Lemay had a rude awakening three weeks ago when he interrupted a police officer who was ticketing his vehicle. "I told the officer that nobody would steal my old car," Lemay explains. "When he gave me a ticket anyway, I was livid."

5 The most common excuse for breaking laws is simple convenience. When there is heavy traffic, Viviana Chelos uses the carpool lane even though she is alone. Chelos, a window dresser in a department store, owns an old mannequin. She places it in the back seat so that the police think she has a passenger. Chelos claims that she isn't hurting anybody. Eric Moore also breaks rules when it's convenient. He regularly drives along the shoulder of the road. "Almost daily, there is a long line of cars waiting at the red light near my home. I would have to be an idiot if I sat in the traffic waiting to get to the turning lane. If I can make it to the turning lane by using the shoulder, why shouldn't I? I actually speed up traffic for others who want to go through the light."

6 Some lawbreakers have original excuses for ignoring traffic rules. When David Shoenbrun visited France, he took a taxi from the Quai d'Orsay toward Avenue Bosquet. His taxi driver sped through two red lights. When they safely arrived at their destination, Shoenbrun scolded the driver about going through red lights. The taxi driver, however, was unrepentant. "What would you have me do? Should I stop like a dumb animal because an automatic, brainless machine turns red every forty seconds?" he argued.

7 Are traffic laws the glue that holds a civilized society together, or are they an annoyance that clear-thinking individuals should ignore? Police officers will argue that traffic laws reduce accidents. Insurance companies point out that when some people break laws and contribute to accidents or car thefts, everyone pays with higher insurance rates. Ultimately, each citizen must decide if obeying a law is the right thing to do.

Sources: *As France Goes* by David Shoenbrun
"Seatbelt Cops Get an Earful" by Matt Helms
"When the Legal Thing Isn't the Right Thing" by Deborah Mead

Vocabulary •• Using Context Clues

1• What is a *jaywalker* (Paragraph 2)? _____

_____

2• Find a word in Paragraph 3 that means "money that you pay as punishment."

_____

3• In Paragraph 4, what is the meaning of *livid*?

    a) happy   **b)** alone   **c)** extremely angry

4• Define *carpool* (Paragraph 5). _____

_____

5• In Paragraph 5, what is a *mannequin*?

    a) a beautiful woman

    b) an animal

    c) a plastic model of a human being

6• Find a word in Paragraph 5 that means "the edge or side of the road, outside the white line."

_____

Ask and Answer Questions

Combine the words in parentheses to compose each question. Sometimes you must add an auxiliary such as *do, does,* or *did.* Then answer each question.

    Example: Why (Guzman, jaywalk) _____*does Guzman jaywalk*_____?

        Answer: _____*He thinks he can cross safely.*_____

7• What (Guzman's job, be) _____

    Answer: _____

8• When (Sahr, receive) _____ a $120 fine?

    Answer: _____

9• Three weeks ago, why (Lemay, become) _____ angry?

    Answer: _____

10• What (Chelos, do) _____ for a living?

    Answer: _____

11• Why (Chelos, sometimes, put) _____ a mannequin in her car?

    Answer: _____

12 • Why (Moore, drive) _____ on the shoulder of the road?

Answer: _____

13 • When Shoenbrun visited France, why (the taxi driver, go)_____

_____ through red lights?

Answer: _____

To develop your listening skills, visit the companion website.

Identify Main Ideas

14 • Look in the introduction. Highlight the thesis statement. (The thesis sums up the main idea of the essay.)

15 • Look in body Paragraphs 2 to 6. Underline the topic sentence in each paragraph. (The topic sentence explains what the paragraph is about.)

 **Watching** •• Road Rage

Reporter Adrienne Arsenault looks into road rage in Canada.

Pre-Watching Vocabulary

Before you listen, read the following definitions.

- *lane:*   a route or path; a road may have several lanes
- *keep your cool:*   remain composed; not become angry
- *rotten:*   very bad
- *driver's licence:*   permit to drive
- *tailgate:*   follow another driver too closely
- *cut someone off:*   suddenly change lanes and drive in front of somebody, forcing the other car to slow down

Watching Comprehension

| cool |
| cut |
| ignore |
| licence |
| rotten |
| weeks |

1 • Fill in the missing words of the narrator. Choose from the words in the box.

George Winchuk has a confession. Once upon a time he was a _____ driver, a poster boy for road rage. That ended quickly on a July night in 1992 when a woman _____ him off. It was an accident that put him in a coma for eight _____. He spent the next five years coping with brain damage. He's now working on getting back his driver's _____ with the help of a special private instructor who teaches him how to keep his _____. "The number-one step is just _____ it. Try not to make eye contact with the driver."

2 • What is road rage? _____

3 • Why did three men beat up Toronto driver Daniel Rosanova?

a) He made a bad lane change.

b) He was tailgating.

c) He cut off the other driver.

4 • According to the video, what is causing road rage? Choose three answers.

☐ congestion (too many drivers on the road)

☐ alcohol

☐ slow drivers

☐ working world that focuses on speed

☐ anonymity of driving

5 • Which Canadian city has more cars per capita than Los Angeles (LA)?

a) Toronto   **b)** Vancouver   **c)** Calgary

6 • Many people call the Toronto police about drivers behaving badly. About how many calls per week do the police get?

a) 100   **b)** 300   **c)** 500

7 • What are highway rangers trained to do?

a) catch speeding drivers

b) help people in accidents that were caused by road rage

c) catch and lecture road ragers

Speaking ·· Danger on the Roads

Work with another student. Discuss dangerous activities on the road.

	PEDESTRIANS	BICYCLE RIDERS	CAR DRIVERS
What laws do they break?			
What dangerous things do they do?			

Listening

Form Questions

You will hear the exact answers to information questions. Try to form a question based on those answers. After you make your own question, you will hear the correct question form. Try to form the question *before* you hear the correct form.

Example: You hear: *To Mexico. She went to Mexico.*
You ask, *Where did she go?*
You will then hear the correct question form: *Where did she go?*

After you hear the correct question, write the question word and the auxiliary in the blanks.

Example: ___*Where*___ ___*did*___ she go?

1. _____ _____ it cost for a plane ticket to London?

2. _____ _____ she leave for work?

3. _____ _____ she going?

4. _____ _____ they live?

5. _____ _____ they laughing?

6. _____ _____ the train leave?

7. _____ _____ she travel with?

8. _____ _____ they break the law?

9. _____ _____ he stay last week?

10. _____ _____ he in prison?

Form Negatives

You will hear a short sentence. Make each sentence negative, and write the contracted verb in the space. Then you will hear the correct negative sentence. Remember to make a guess before you hear the correct negative form.

Example: We ___*don't like*___ pizza.

1. She _____ many mistakes.

2. He _____ too fast.

3. We _____ late for class yesterday.

4. Carol _____ her homework every night.

5. Richard _____ his homework last night.

6. He _____ many problems.

7. Last Thursday, he _____ a problem.

8. It _____ soon.

9. Right now, it _____.

10. Yesterday, it _____.

Listening The Legal Drinking Age

Dr. Marcia Nixon is an anthropologist. In the interview, Dr. Nixon discusses the legal drinking age. Listen to the audio recording and then answer the following questions.

Listening for Main Ideas

1 • Indicate which three topics Dr. Nixon discusses:

☑ the drinking ages across Canada

☑ the reasons why some people become alcoholics

☐ drinking rituals in Africa and Asia

☐ the Uniform Drinking Age Act in the United States

☑ why smoking is popular among North American teens

☐ drinking habits in some European countries

Listening for Details

2 • What is the legal drinking age in most Canadian provinces? ___19___

3 • How many provinces have a legal age of eighteen?

a) one   **b)** two   **c)** three   **d)** four

4 • Which provinces have a legal drinking age of eighteen? _____
___manitoba, Québec, Alberta___

5 • What is the legal drinking age in most US states? ___21___

6 • In the United States, what is the Uniform Drinking Age Act?
___a loose money___

7 • How does the Uniform Drinking Age Act punish certain states? _____
_____

8 • What is Dr. Nixon's main point? Choose the best answer.

☐ The legal drinking age should be eighteen years old.

☑ In North America, we should treat alcohol as a part of life. Then it won't seem so dangerous and exciting for young people.

☐ The legal drinking age is lower in Canada than in the United States.

Discussion

1 • Should the legal drinking age be higher or lower?

2 • Should the government eliminate the legal drinking age?

To perfect your reading skills, visit the companion website.

Written Response

Write a paragraph about your past experiences with the drinking age. Did you and your friends drink before you reached the legal age? Why or why not?

Writing Past Tense Verbs

Only double the last letter of regular verbs that end in a consonant-vowel-consonant combination.

stop – sto**pp**ed   plan – pla**nn**ed

If the verb ends in -*e*, or if it contains two vowels, do not double the last letter.

hope – hoped   rain – rained

A list of irregular past tense verbs appears in the appendix of *Open Book English Grammar*.

Speaking ·· Innocent or Guilty?

Join a team of students. Pretend that last night, at 9 p.m., a local business was robbed. Some students in your classroom are suspects. Some of you will be the investigators, and some of you will be the suspects.

If you are the suspects, you and your team members must come up with an alibi. Imagine that you were all together last night. Decide where you were and what you were doing at the time of the crime.

The students in the class will interrogate the suspects, one by one, to compare their stories. The "investigators" must look for inconsistencies in the stories.

Reading

Reading 8.3

The following essay examines how crime shows influence jurors. As you read, underline or highlight words that you do not understand.

Pre-Reading Vocabulary

Place the following words in the correct spaces. Use each word once.

juror	jury	trial	defence lawyer
prosecutor	judge	scientists	scientific

1 • Forensic _____ inspect the evidence at a crime scene.

They gather _____ evidence. Sometimes they present

the evidence in a criminal _____.

2 • At each trial, the _____ works for the government and

must convince the judge and _____ that the suspect is

guilty. The _____ defends the suspect.

The _____ listens to both sides and gives instructions

to the jury. Each _____, or member of the jury, listens

carefully to the evidence.

The *CSI* Effect
by Richard Willing

1 Television shows such as *CSI* (*Crime Scene Investigation*) are affecting action in courthouses by, among other things, raising jurors' expectations of what prosecutors should produce at trial. Prosecutors, defence lawyers, and judges call it "the *CSI* effect," after the crime-scene shows that are among the hottest attractions on television. The shows feature high-tech labs and gorgeous techies. By shining a glamorous light on a gory profession, the programs also have helped to draw more students into forensic studies.

2 The programs also foster what analysts say is the mistaken notion that criminal science is fast and infallible and always gets its man. That's affecting the way lawyers prepare their cases, as well as the expectations that police and the public place on real crime labs. Real crime-scene investigators say that because of the programs, people often have unrealistic ideas of what criminal science can deliver.

3 Many lawyers, judges, and legal consultants say they appreciate how *CSI*-type shows have increased interest in forensic evidence. "Talking about science in the courtroom used to be like talking about geometry—a real jury turnoff," says jury consultant Robert Hirschhorn of Lewisville, Texas. "Now that there's this obsession with the shows, you can talk to jurors about scientific evidence and just see from the looks on their faces that they find it fascinating."

4 But some defence lawyers say *CSI* and similar shows make jurors rely too heavily on scientific findings. Prosecutors also have complaints. They say the shows can make it more difficult for them to win convictions in the large majority of cases in which scientific evidence is irrelevant or absent.

5 Lawyers and judges say the *CSI* effect has become a phenomenon in courthouses across the nation. For example, in Phoenix, jurors in a murder trial noticed that a bloody coat introduced as evidence had not been tested for DNA. The jurors alerted the judge. The tests were unnecessary because, early in the trial, the defendant admitted his presence at the murder scene. The judge decided that TV had taught jurors about DNA tests, but not enough about when to use them.

6 Juries are sometimes right to expect high-tech evidence. Three years ago in Richmond, Virginia, jurors in a murder trial asked the judge whether a cigarette butt found during the investigation could be tested for links to the defendant. Defence attorneys had ordered DNA tests but had not yet introduced them into evidence. The jury's hunch was correct—the tests **exonerated** the defendant, and the jury **acquitted** him.

exonerated
cleared

acquitted
determined that he
was not guilty

7 Some of the science on crime shows is state-of-the-art. Real lab technicians can, for example, lift DNA profiles from cigarette butts, candy wrappers and gobs of spit, just as their Hollywood counterparts do. But some of what's on TV is far-fetched. Real technicians don't pour caulk into

knife wounds to make a cast of the weapon. That wouldn't work in soft tissue. Machines that can identify cologne from scents on clothing are still in the experimental phase. A criminal charge based on "neuro-linguistic programming"—detecting lies by the way a person's eyes shift—likely would be dismissed by a judge.

8 Real scientists say the main problem with crime shows is that the science is always above reproach. "You never see a case where the sample is degraded or the lab work is faulty or the test results don't solve the crime," says Dan Krane, president and DNA specialist at Forensic Bioinformatics in Fairborn, Ohio. "These things happen all the time in the real world."

Write Questions

On a piece of paper, write ten questions about this reading. Leave space for the answers. Your questions should include at least three verb tenses, and one question should contain a modal auxiliary such as *can, should,* or *must*. On the back of your paper, put the answers to each question.

You can make some questions about vocabulary and some about content. Remember to use the proper question word order. Then exchange papers with a classmate and answer your classmate's questions.

Tip Grammar

Question Form
Ensure that your questions have the proper word order.

Question word	+	Auxiliary	+	Subject	+	Verb	+	Rest of sentence
Why		do		people		watch		crime shows?

Writing Topics

Write about one of the following topics. When you finish writing, refer to the relevant checklist on the inside back cover.

1 • Explain why there should or should not be a legal drinking age.

2 • Write about a good or bad driving experience. You can describe an experience when you were the driver or the passenger. Explain what happened.

3 • Give your opinion of crime shows and movies. Do you like shows about crimes or criminals? Why or why not?

4 • Describe some laws that are not fair. Explain why the laws are not good.

5 • Write an essay about the dangerous things that people do on our roads. You should write an introduction, two body paragraphs, and a conclusion. For your body paragraphs, you can write about any of the following groups of people: pedestrians, bicycle riders, motorcycle drivers, or car drivers.

To review some of the vocabulary studied in this chapter, visit the companion website.

WritingWorkshop
Writing a Paragraph

Generating Ideas

When you are given a writing assignment, you might not have ideas for how to develop it. Also, sometimes the teacher may give you a topic that is large, and you must make it more narrow and specific. There are various strategies that you can use to find ideas. Two common strategies are **freewriting** and **brainstorming**.

When you **freewrite**, you write without stopping for a limited period of time. You record whatever thoughts come into your mind without worrying about spelling, grammar, or punctuation.

EXAMPLE

What is the value of part-time work? I've only worked in a restaurant. Schedules are good for college students. Can work nights or weekends. Serving people is so different from studying. You can relax your brain and go on automatic pilot. But you have to remember people's orders so it can be hard. And some customers are rude. What else? The tips can be very good.

When you **brainstorm**, you create a list of ideas. You don't worry about grammar or spelling—the point is to generate ideas.

EXAMPLE

Topic: Tipping of service workers
- They need tips to pay their bills.
- Tips show appreciation for hard work.
- Who should we tip?
- Taxi drivers? Hair shampooist?
- Tips are expensive for the customer.
- No one knows exactly how much to give.

Compose It ·· Generate Ideas

Use freewriting or brainstorming to generate ideas about one of the following topics. Your teacher might suggest some other topics. The questions beside each topic are some ideas you can think about.

Habits: What are your good and bad habits? How can you stop a bad habit?

Stress: What are some reasons why students feel stressed? What are the best ways to relax and reduce stress?

Work: Should students have part-time jobs? What is the value of part-time work?

Other Topics: _____

The Topic Sentence

A **paragraph** is the main building block of most types of writing. It has one main idea, and the other sentences in the paragraph support the main idea. Present the main idea in a **topic sentence**. Your topic sentence should have the following qualities.

- It is the most general sentence in the paragraph.
- It expresses the **topic**.
- It has a **main idea** that expresses the focus of the paragraph.

    topic   +   main idea

My lab partner <u>has many interesting qualities.</u>

Writing Exercise 1

Read the following paragraphs. Then choose the best topic sentence.

1. When a person undergoes a period of high stress, it can lead to insomnia. Insomnia can also be caused by high alcohol consumption; although alcohol makes it easier to fall asleep, the quality of the sleep is reduced. To minimize insomnia, a person should have a regular bedtime and a regular wake-up time.

   Possible topic sentences:

   ☐ Many people in the world get insomnia.

   ☐ Insomnia, the inability to have prolonged deep sleep, is caused by several factors.

   ☐ Insomnia is the inability to have prolonged, deep sleep.

   ☐ I will explain the causes of insomnia.

2. We expect our lives to follow the pattern of such stories. We grow up believing that love will just happen, without effort. We become convinced that we will only find happiness once we find a soulmate, and we expect this soulmate to fulfill all of our needs and to feel eternally lustful toward us.

   Possible topic sentences:

   ☐ Fairy tales give us unrealistic expectations about love.

   ☐ I think that relationships are complicated.

   ☐ Through stories, we learn that love never dies.

   ☐ Love is a great thing.

Tip

Topic Sentence Problems

Your topic sentence must make a point. It should not be vague. Do not write *My topic is* or *I will write about.*

Vague:	This is a big problem. (What is a problem? The topic is unclear.)
No main idea:	I will talk about bicycle riders. (What is the main point? This says nothing relevant about the topic.)
Good topic sentence:	Bicycle riders break many traffic laws.

Writing Exercise 2

Write "OK" under good topic sentences. If the sentence is vague, incomplete, or without a focus, rewrite it.

1• I will write about my lab partner.

_____

2• Some traffic laws are not reasonable.

_____

3• There are some bad habits.

_____

4• Many great artists had difficult lives.

_____

5• I will talk about stress.

_____

6• This is my dream job.

_____

Compose It ·· Write Topic Sentences

Write a topic sentence for two of the following topics. You might want to refer to your topics in the previous Compose It section. Remember to give your topic a more narrow and specific focus.

Habits   **Stress**   **Work**

EXAMPLE ——— Topic: _Work_   Narrowed topic: _Tipping of service workers_ _____
Topic sentence: _The rules about tipping are not clear._ _____

1• Topic: _____   Narrowed topic: _____

Topic sentence: _____

_____

2• Topic: _____   Narrowed topic: _____

Topic sentence: _____

_____

The Supporting Ideas

When you finish writing a topic sentence, you must think of specific evidence that supports it. You can add facts, anecdotes, reasons, examples, and statistics.

Topic Sentence

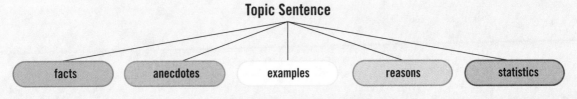

facts   anecdotes   examples   reasons   statistics

Writing a Paragraph ·· **WRITING WORKSHOP 1**

Writing Exercise 3

Read the paragraph below and do the following tasks.

1• Highlight the topic sentence.

2• Number the supporting arguments.

3• Underline the concluding sentence.

Major scientific breakthroughs are always made by scientists with university degrees, right? Wrong! In fact, many breakthroughs in math and science are made by amateurs. For example, in 1996, a nine-year-old schoolgirl designed an experiment that challenged the healing-touch notion among the alternative-medicine community. After trying her simple experiment, the healers were correct just 44 percent of the time. In another case, a housewife from San Diego discovered new geometric shapes of non-repetitive patterns that could join perfectly on a surface. Scientists thought that all of the possibilities were known, but the housewife proved them wrong. Benjamin Franklin was a statesman who discovered that lightning is electricity. Scientific breakthroughs can be made by amateurs with intense curiosity and a fresh approach to analyzing a problem.

Writing Exercise 4

Put a checkmark beside each sentence that could be included in a paragraph about bad driving habits.

Topic sentence: People have several bad driving habits.

☐ Some drivers slide through stop signs and do not come to a complete stop.

☐ Children watch videos in cars.

☐ When drivers forget to check over their shoulder before changing lanes, they can cause an accident.

☐ Passengers in cars sometimes throw cigarettes out of the window.

☐ About 40 percent of drivers follow other cars too closely.

☐ Nathan took his driving test five times before he passed.

☐ Some drivers refuse to let other drivers move into the space in front of them.

☐ Aggressive drivers cause accidents when they speed or cut other cars off.

Revise for Unity

A good topic sentence unifies the paragraph. The topic sentence should be general enough that all of the details and examples in the paragraph relate back to it. Don't include facts in your paragraph that have nothing to do with the topic sentence.

Writing Exercise 5

As you read the paragraph below, do the following tasks.

1 • Underline the topic sentence.

2 • Cross out sentences that do not support the topic sentence.

My father watches too much television. When I was a child, my dad got home from work and then went to see what was on TV. Later, while the rest of us ate supper in the kitchen, he would take his plate to the living room and watch the news. On weekends, he watched sports, and we heard him yelling every time his team's players made a mistake. Of course, many television shows are very bad. It is a waste of time to watch them. I really hate reality TV shows. Today my father is an old man, and the television is still his constant companion.

Compose It •• Write a Stand-Alone Paragraph

Compose a paragraph about one of the following topics. Ensure that your paragraph has a topic sentence and supporting facts and examples. Also, ensure that it is unified. Every sentence should relate to the topic sentence.

Habits   Stress   Work

Other Topics: _____

WritingWorkshop

Writing an Essay

2

The Essay

An **essay** is divided into three parts: an **introduction**, a **body**, and a **conclusion**. Look at the following example to see how different types of paragraphs form an essay. The essential elements of the essay are highlighted.

EXAMPLE

The **introduction** begins with general statements about the topic.

Real-Life Heroes

Children idolize superheroes such as Batman, Superman, or Buffy the Vampire Slayer. The superhero stage is followed by the "I want to be famous" stage, when adolescents start trying to shoot like Michael Jordan, act like Al Pacino, or sing like Mariah Carey. These fantasy heroes get all of the attention when there are true heroes in our cities. **The public should pay more attention to real-life heroes.**

The **thesis statement** tells the reader what the essay is about.

Each body paragraph begins with a topic sentence.

Those who work in public safety risk their lives to rescue others. When a building is consumed with fire, brave firefighters save trapped occupants. During the terrorist attacks of 9/11, many firefighters lost their lives when they tried to rescue trapped civilians. Without police officers, citizens would live in constant fear of attack. Regular men and women patrol our streets and help make us all safer.

Each **body paragraph** contains details that support the thesis statement.

Medical staff and researchers cure diseases and save lives. When a new epidemic arrives, people panic and rush to hospitals. During the first years of AIDS and SARS, medical personnel risked their own lives to treat the sick. Researchers do painstaking work to find cures for such diseases. Many people owe their lives to such heroic individuals.

The **concluding paragraph** restates the main idea. It ends with a suggestion or prediction.

Our cities have many courageous people who selflessly work in hazardous conditions. Police officers, firefighters, and medical personnel work hard, often for modest wages, to protect the public. Instead of focusing on celebrities and superheroes, students should learn about the heroes among us.

The Thesis Statement

When you plan an essay, the first thing you must do is decide what your essay will be about. The **thesis statement** is a sentence that expresses the main idea of an essay. Look at the following thesis statements.

Citizens can help the environment by making some simple changes.
Some video games promote violence.

How is a thesis statement different from a topic sentence?

The thesis statement is similar to a topic sentence. They both express a main idea. However, a thesis statement has a larger focus than a topic sentence. The thesis statement explains what the essay is about. Then each topic sentence supports the thesis statement.

EXAMPLE —

Thesis statement: Celebrations help people in several ways.

1) Topic sentence: When people enter a new life stage, the celebration brings families together.

2) Topic sentence: Religious holidays and festivals help families feel like part of the community.

Thesis Statement Checklist

A thesis statement must have the following qualities.

- **It is a complete statement.** Your thesis should have a subject and a verb and express a complete idea.

  Incomplete: The best things about travelling.

  Thesis: Travelling teaches us about other cultures.

- **It expresses a clear topic and a main idea.** Ensure that your thesis statement expresses a point of view or attitude. Avoid phrases such as *My topic is* and *I will write about*.

  Vague: I had a big problem.
  (The topic is unclear.)

  No main idea: I will discuss my car accident.
  (This sentence has no focus and says nothing relevant about the topic.)

  Thesis: My car accident changed my life.

Writing Exercise 1

Examine each statement. If it is a good thesis statement, write *TS* on the line. Write *X* next to weak thesis statements. Discuss what the problems are with the weak statements.

EXAMPLE —   I will talk about driving. _____X_____

1 • The high cost of student housing. _____

2 • In this paper, I will discuss my job. _____

3 • Some musicians are very bad role models. _____

4 • The problems with tattoos. _____

5 • This changed my life. _____

6 • Art courses teach students important skills. _____

7 • I will write about my classmate. _____

8 • My classmate followed several trends when she was a child. _____

Writing Exercise 2

Write a thesis statement for each group of supporting ideas. Ensure that your thesis statement is complete.

EXAMPLE — Thesis: *When you buy a car, make an informed decision.*

a) Ask family members what type of car would be most useful.

b) Determine how much money you can afford to pay for the car.

c) Do research on the Internet about the specific types of cars that you are interested in.

1 • Thesis: _____

_____

a) Most people under twenty-five years of age simply vote like their parents or friends.

b) To make an informed choice during an election, people need to have life experiences, which include paying rent and bills.

c) Twenty-five-year-olds are also less likely to be manipulated by politicians because they have a stronger sense of what they want.

2 • Thesis: _____

_____

a) First, I do not smoke because I grew up in a household full of smokers.

b) My grandmother's death from lung cancer also provided me with a strong lesson about smoking.

c) I was lucky to have friends in school who also didn't smoke, so I never felt strong peer pressure to pick up the habit.

3 • Thesis: _____

_____

a) The soup was tasteless, and I forgot to add the salt.

b) I served my guests the meat, and when they cut into it, I realized the meat was not well cooked.

c) When I made the dessert, I accidentally used unsweetened chocolate in the sauce, and it tasted terrible.

Compose It ·· Write Thesis Statements

Write two thesis statements. You can write both statements about one topic, or you can choose different topics. Remember to give your topic a more narrow and specific focus.

| Trend | Art | Celebration | Travel | Driving |

Other Topics: _____

EXAMPLE ──┬ Topic: _*Travel*_ Narrowed topic: _*reasons to travel*_____
          └ Thesis statement: _*People travel for several reasons.*_____

1• Topic: _____ Narrowed topic: _____

Thesis statement: _____

_____

2• Topic: _____ Narrowed topic: _____

Thesis statement: _____

_____

The Introduction

The **introductory paragraph** introduces the subject of your essay. It helps your reader understand why you are writing the text. The thesis statement is the last sentence in your introduction.

Sample Introduction

Canada is a materialistic nation. At a young age, children watch commercials about breakfast cereals and toys, and they learn to desire those items. In fact, the average child sees thousands of advertisements before the age of six. **Advertisers have too much influence in our culture.**

── General information

── Thesis statement

Introduction Styles

You can introduce your essay in several ways.

- **General background:** You can write a few general sentences about the topic.

- **Historical background:** You can give some historical information about the topic.

- **Anecdote:** You can tell a true story about something that happened. Your story should relate to the topic.

End your introduction with the thesis statement, which expresses the main point of the essay.

Writing Exercise 3

In the following introductions, the thesis statement is in bold. Decide what introduction style each writer uses.

1• In the past, people traded items to get what they needed. Someone might exchange a cow for a wagon. Later, silver and gold were formed into coins. Because the coins could be traded for products or land, people desired them. Today, we are a money-obsessed nation. Everybody wants a big house, a nice car, and a vacation by a beach. **However, to be truly happy, do not make money the focus of your life**.

Style: a) general   b) historical   c) anecdotal

2• Kurt Cobain became an international music star when he was in his early twenties. The CD *Nevermind*, which he made with his band Nirvana, became very popular. However, Cobain disliked the attention. Friends said that he was embarrassed by the limousines and the wealth. Ultimately, his addiction to painkillers and to powerful narcotics contributed to his decision to end his life. **Fame does not make people happy.**

Style: a) general   b) historical   c) anecdotal

3• Many students choose colleges that are distant from their homes. For the first time in their lives, they must move out and find an apartment. This is a big step, because students must learn to cook, clean, and manage their own finances. They must also learn to live with roommates. **It is very exciting to move out of home for the first time.**

Style: a) general   b) historical   c) anecdotal

Writing Exercise 4

Read the paragraphs below. Highlight the topic sentence in body paragraphs 1 and 2. (Look for sentences that express the main idea of each paragraph.) Then write an introduction. You can begin with an anecdote, historical information, or general information. End your introduction with a thesis statement.

Add an Introduction

Body paragraph 1: First, let the dog know that you are the boss. Animals in social units have a hierarchy. Dogs, like many other mammals, often want to be a leader. If you are not clearly positioned as the master, and if you feel a little insecure in the role, a puppy can become a dog that bites, attacks others, and destroys property simply because it thinks that it is the boss. Dogs feel more secure when they know that someone else is in control.

Body paragraph 2: Second, plan to give your dog some time and attention. Dogs don't bathe themselves. Someone has to do it. Dogs need to be taken on walks daily, in good weather and bad. And remember, it is cruel and inhumane to keep a large dog locked up in a city apartment all day. Dogs are not ornaments. They need attention, fresh air, and adequate exercise.

Conclusion: Remember that owning a pet is a responsibility. If you are not willing to give your dog time and attention, then you should not buy a pet.

Compose It ·· Write an Introduction

Choose one of your thesis statements from the Compose It section on page 131 and then, on a separate sheet of paper, write an introduction for your topic.

The Supporting Ideas

In an essay, each body paragraph provides supporting evidence for the thesis statement.

Introduction

The **thesis statement** identifies the main idea of the essay.

》》》

Body paragraph

The **topic sentence** identifies the main idea of the supporting paragraph.

- **Facts**
- **Statistics**
- **Anecdotes**
- **Relevant quotations**

Writing Exercise 5

Read the essay and then do the following tasks.

- First, underline the thesis statement.

- Then write a topic sentence at the beginning of each body paragraph. The topic sentence should sum up the main point of the paragraph in an interesting way.

Introduction

In past centuries, people visiting distant nations became ill because of new viruses. Pirates on the high seas attacked passing ships. Land travellers were not much safer. Thieves could attack wagons and trains. Today, travel is quick and relatively risk-free. Nonetheless, there are still certain hazards inherent in travelling. There are several things you should do to ensure that you have a safe trip.

Body paragraph 1
Topic sentence: _____

_____

For example, before you arrive in a new town, find an address and phone number of affordable lodging, and even book a room for your first night. If you are a budget traveller, you can always find cheaper accommodations the next day. Also, make sure that you have a map of your destination. You can download maps on the Internet.

➡

Body paragraph 2
Topic sentence: _____

_____

You could bring along a first-aid kit that includes bandages and pain relievers. Also, wear hats in very hot places. If you are visiting a tropical country, make sure you have the proper vaccinations. Be careful about where and what you eat, and buy bottled drinking water. Your health is important. Obviously, if you get sick, you are not going to enjoy your trip.

Conclusion

If you take risks with your health, if you are careless with your money and passport, or if you underestimate thieves, you may have unpleasant experiences when you travel. Of course, if you are careful, you should have a perfectly safe and exciting trip.

Compose It ·· List Supporting Ideas

Choose one of your thesis statements from the Compose It section on page 131 and then, on a separate sheet of paper, brainstorm a list of supporting ideas for your topic.

EXAMPLE ——— People travel for several reasons
- too much stress at work
- time with the family
- learn about cultures
- eat exotic foods
- try new sports and activities
- practise another language

The Conclusion

You can conclude your essay by rephrasing your main points. Then you can end with a suggestion or a prediction. For example, the essay "Real-Life Heroes" on page 128 ends with a suggestion.

The following conclusion ends an essay about cellphone etiquette.

Remind the reader of your main points.	In conclusion, cellphone users do not show enough respect to the people around them. They speak loudly in public places. They download loud and annoying cellphone rings, and they answer their phones in movie theatres and classrooms.
End with a prediction or suggestion.	Parents should teach their children about cellphone etiquette.

Transitional Words and Expressions

Transitional words and expressions help the reader follow the logic of a text.

If you are unfamiliar with an expression, write a definition or translation beside it.

CHRONOLOGY (Sequence of ideas)	CONTRAST	ADDITIONAL ARGUMENT
• first,* second, third • next • then • finally	• although • however • on the other hand	• additionally • also • as well • in addition • furthermore

*Do not write *firstly*.

EXAMPLE	EMPHASIS	CONCLUDING IDEAS
• for example • for instance	• above all • clearly • in fact • more importantly	• finally • in conclusion • in short • therefore • to conclude

Writing Exercise 6

Write definitions or translations for the expressions below.

1 • however _____

2 • although _____

3 • furthermore _____

4 • clearly _____

5 • above all _____

6 • in short _____

7 • therefore _____

8 • on the other hand _____

9 • in fact _____

10 • in conclusion _____

Writing Exercise 7

Read the following paragraph. Underline the most appropriate transitional expressions.

Last year, one hundred factory workers were questioned about lotteries. Ninety people said that they buy lottery tickets (furthermore / even though / clearly) they do not have extra money. (In fact / However / Therefore) one worker said, "I really can't afford it, but I buy the tickets anyway." (On the other hand / Furthermore / Finally), some of the people in the group spend more than five hundred dollars per year on lottery tickets. (On the other hand / Furthermore / Finally), someone in this country becomes a millionaire every month, and if people don't buy lottery tickets, they won't have the possibility of winning. (Second / However / Above all), everyone should remember that the chances of being hit by lightning are much higher than the chances of winning the lottery. (Then / However / In conclusion) people may dream of a lottery win, but the dream rarely becomes reality. (For instance / Therefore / Also) if you spend money on lottery tickets, be realistic. You probably won't win.

The Essay Plan

A plan is a visual map that shows the essay's main and supporting ideas. It also includes details for each supporting idea.

Sample Essay Plan

Thesis statement: People travel for two main reasons.

   I: They need to get away and relax.
      Support: Maybe they have too much stress at work.
        Detail: My parents work very long hours and they need a break.
      Support: They want to spend time with the family.
        Detail: Our family goes to the lake every summer.

   II: They want to learn about other cultures.
      Support: They can practise a new language.
        Detail: When we went to Cancun, we practised Spanish.
      Support: They can eat new types of food.
        Detail: We loved the mole, tortillas, and other treats in Mexico.
Concluding suggestion: Everybody should travel to different places.

Compose It ·· Create an Essay Plan

Develop an essay plan for one of the following topics.
You can choose ideas that you have developed in this workshop.

Trend   Art   Celebration   Travel   Driving

Other topics: _____

Introduction

Thesis statement: _____

_____

Body paragraph 1

Topic sentence: _____

_____

    Support: _____

    Details: _____

_____

    Support: _____

    Details: _____

_____

Body paragraph 2

Topic sentence: _____

_____

    Support: _____

    Details: _____

_____

    Support: _____

    Details: _____

_____

Conclusion
(Think of a final suggestion or prediction.) _____

_____

_____

Appendix

Oral Presentations

There are a few points to remember when you make an oral presentation.

Plan Your Presentation

- **Structure your presentation.** Include an appealing introduction. Use facts or examples to support your main points. Make sure you have a conclusion.
- **Practise.** Your teacher will not be impressed if you frequently pause to think of something to say, or if you constantly search through your notes.
- **Don't memorize your presentation** or you'll sound unnatural. It is better to speak to the audience and occasionally refer to your notes than to rattle off a memorized text.
- **Time yourself.** Ensure that your oral presentation respects the specified time limit.
- **Use cue cards.** On cue cards, only write down key words and phrases. If you write your entire presentation on cue cards, you could end up getting confused and losing your place. Look at the example provided.

Presentation Text	Cue Card
The apple slicer is a very useful new product. It cuts apples with one movement. It is extremely convenient. You no longer need to use a knife or cutting board.	*apple slicer* *one movement* *no knife or cutting board*

Give Your Presentation

- Look at your entire audience, not just the teacher.
- Don't read. However, you can use cue cards to guide yourself through the presentation.
- When the assignment requires it, bring in visual or audio supports. These can make your presentation more interesting.

Appendix

Television Journal

To improve your listening skills, watch an English-language television program each week. Find a program that tells a story. You will then write about the TV show in the form of a journal entry.

Your journal entry should contain the following information:

- The title of the show
- The date you watched the show
- The names of the main characters
- A short summary of the show: describe what happened. If you don't understand everything in the show, try to describe what happened to one particular character.
- Six questions that you would like to ask the show's writer

Your journal entry should look like this:

Title of the show: Lost

Characters: Sawyer, Kate, Jack, Anna Lucia

Time and date: Monday, September 4th, 8 p.m.

Summary

Sawyer was one of four survivors of a plane crash. He was shot at and almost died in the show. His wound did not heal and he had a fever. Walking through the forest with his companions, he fell and lost consciousness. A woman in the group, Anna Lucia, did not want to help Sawyer, but when the others insisted, she let them carry him to safety and find a doctor to treat his wound.

Questions

1. Why did the plane crash?   2. Where is the island?

Tip Grammar

Television Show Titles
When you write the title of a television show, capitalize the first letter of the first word as well as that of all the main words. Also, underline the title.

Example: We used to watch <u>The Sopranos</u> every week.
I sometimes watch <u>The Young and the Restless</u>.

Appendix

Vocabulary Boost: The Body

ankle
cheek
chin
elbow
eyebrow
eyelashes
forehead
heel
hip
knee
knuckle
neck
shoulder
thigh
thumb
toe
waist
wrist

Label the body parts using the words provided.

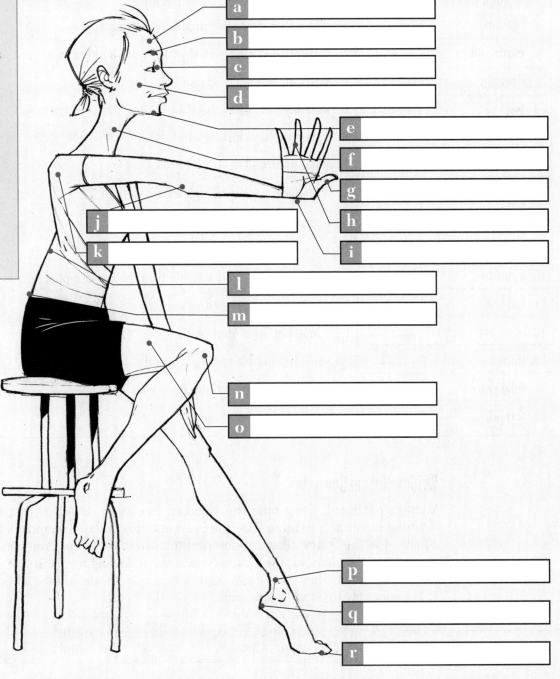

a

b

c

d

e

f

g

j

h

k

i

l

m

n

o

p

q

r

Appendix

Vocabulary Boost: The Weather

4

Write the letter of the correct definition next to each weather term.

WEATHER TERMS		DEFINITIONS
1. blizzard	_____	a. water that rises and spreads over land
2. earthquake	_____	b. the entire sky is covered with clouds and the sun is not visible
3. drought	_____	c. misty air, like a cloud that is on the ground
4. fog	_____	d. a flashing of light caused by atmospheric electricity
5. flood	_____	e. a destructive whirling wind
6. forecast	_____	f. hot and humid
7. frost	_____	g. a loud sound that follows a flash of light
8. hail	_____	h. a giant rise of water due to strong winds
9. icicle	_____	i. a covering of ice crystals on a surface
10. lightning	_____	j. a hanging piece of ice made from frozen dripping water
11. muggy	_____	k. a movement of the earth's crust
12. overcast	_____	l. a long period of dry weather
13. thunder	_____	m. small balls of ice that fall from the clouds
14. tidal wave	_____	n. a prediction of weather conditions
15. tornado	_____	o. a storm of blowing snow

Writing Suggestion

Write a paragraph describing the weather this week. Use the past tense to describe yesterday's weather. Use the present tense to describe today's weather. Finally, use the future tense to describe tomorrow's weather. You can use the terms from the chart, and you can also use the following terms. In your report, include some activities people can do. For example, "Today the weather is mild. It is a good day to go for a long walk."

cool	freezing	mild	warm	hot
light winds	strong winds	sunny	cloudy	rain

Appendix

Vocabulary Boost: Items in the Home

blanket
closet
doorknob
dresser
drawer
faucet
handle
hangers
mattress
oven
pillow
pot
railing
rug
sink
stairs
stove

Label each object using the words listed in the chart.

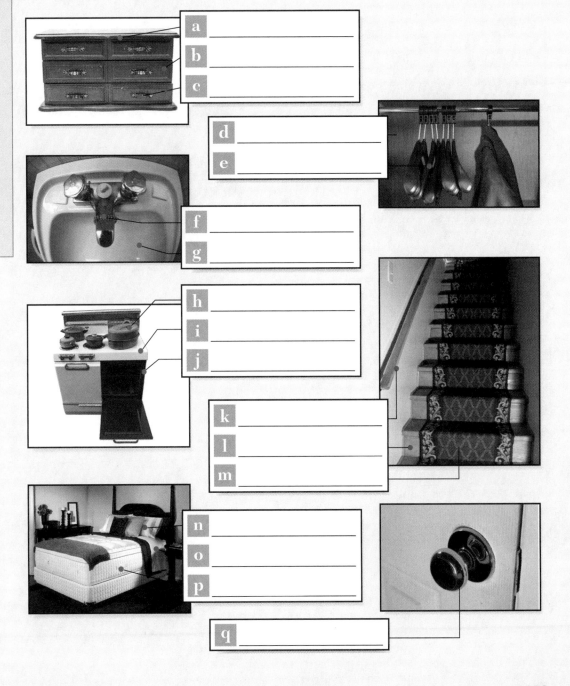

a _____

b _____

c _____

d _____

e _____

f _____

g _____

h _____

i _____

j _____

k _____

l _____

m _____

n _____

o _____

p _____

q _____

Notes

NOTES

NOTES